PRAISE

HOODOO YO[

"Hoodoo Your Love is filled with wisdom the internet will never teach you. Starr Casas is the conjure teacher that we all want and need, and this book is another session immersed in her wisdom. Her conversations about the many layers of love magic are hard truths that will help your love magic find wild success."

> —Jacki Smith author of *Coventry Magic with Candles, Oils, and Herbs*, coauthor of *Do It Yourself Akashic Wisdom*, and founder of Coventry Creations

"Mama Starr Casas is 'old school.' She was doing this work before it became all the rage and she knows what she's talking about. Her style is direct and evocative, and this book is hard to put down. *Hoodoo Your Love* is a valuable addition to any folk magic library."

> —H. Byron Ballard, author of *Seasons of a Magical Life*

"I always learn something new with Starr. In *Hoodoo Your Love*, she generously shares tips, tricks, and wisdom you won't find anywhere else, rooted in her living experience and honoring her elders and ancestors."

> —Christopher Penczak, author of *The Witch's Heart*

"Hoodoo in the southern United States has a legacy of using what was available in the local environment. Mama Starr Casas's *Hoodoo Your Love* demonstrates that folk magic can be performed using materials many may consider mundane. Mama Starr's voice places you on her front porch sipping coffee and listening to her advice and lore. A refreshing insightful look into the wisdom and workings of spiritual workers and their legacy of love working."

> —Tony Kail, cultural anthropologist and author of *A Secret History of Memphis Hoodoo*

"Far more than just a book on managing love through the power of Conjure, *Hoodoo Your Love* is a masterpiece of visceral, authentic Hoodoo that covers the common sense and straight talk so often missed in modern presentations of Conjure. With the authentic voice of a true Conjure woman, Starr Casas pulls no punches as she leads the reader on a frank and powerful journey through all aspects of Hoodoo love work. Never one to shy away from the raw power of real Conjure work, Casas strikes gold again with this latest addition to her library of must-have Hoodoo classics. Through her writing, our souls can remember and relish the feeling of learning Hoodoo at the knee of our elders, an experience that is so often lost in today's world."

—Katrina Rasbold, author of *Crossroads of Conjure, Energy Magic,* and *Uncrossing*

"Containing never before published material, *Hoodoo Your Love* is another classic, true Conjure book by Mama Starr Casas. She keeps the work true to its origins, returning to the roots of Conjure with tips, tricks, and works. From the proper Bible verses to use in a work to learning how to pray and create your petition, Mama Starr shares a lot of good knowledge. I learn something new every time I read the book."

—Charity Bedell (Loona Wynd), coauthor of *The Good Witch's Guide*

"In her characteristic straight-talkin' style, Starr Casas delivers the lowdown on how to magically manage affairs of the heart. From hello to farewell, and every possibility in between, *Hoodoo Your Love* is filled with practical no-nonsense advice and conjure work geared toward all things love. It's a must-have for any lover's bookshelf!"

—Cairelle Crow, coeditor of *Brigid's Light*

HOODOO YOUR LOVE

HOODOO YOUR LOVE

Conjure the Love You Want (and Keep It)
· · · · · · · ·
STARR CASAS

WEISER BOOKS

This edition first published in 2022 by Weiser Books, an imprint of
Red Wheel/Weiser, LLC
With offices at:
65 Parker Street, Suite 7
Newburyport, MA 01950
www.redwheelweiser.com

ISBN: 978-1-57863-755-3
Library of Congress Cataloging-in-Publication Data available upon request.

Cover design by Kathryn Sky-Peck
Cover photograph by David Hoptman/Alamy Stock Photo
Interior by Maureen Forys, Happenstance Type-O-Rama
Typeset in Makclin Slab, Macklin Sans, and Colporteur

Printed in the United States of America
IBI
10 9 8 7 6 5 4 3 2 1

CONTENTS

HOODOO YOUR LOVE

INTRODUCTION

Conjure, also known as Hoodoo—the two names are often used interchangeably and I will do so in this book—focuses on making one's life better; it focuses on the home and hearth, helping folks in everyday living. The main concern of a conjure woman is blessing their homes and keeping the home peaceful, making sure their mate is faithful, drawing luck, and much more. The way Hoodoo achieves these things is by laying tricks or working the root. This is done through prayers, candles, lucky hands, and other means. Dirts, powders, salts, waters, and other ingredients are worked with in order to complete a job. There are many works that have been handed down orally through the ages.

Conjure includes works on healing a broken heart by working with an animal heart and works of healing and love as well as domination and controlling. You'll find all that here and also learn a way of working with a cow's tongue to sweeten someone's words toward you. This book will cover what I call hard works and what others call hexing work. We have to remember all things come into balance—you can't have light without dark. And we also have to remember that Conjure comes from a tradition that had to take justice into its own hands—so it deals with drawing in a lover as well as keeping one honest.

I know some folks don't believe it is right to make someone do something against their will, and that is their right to feel that way. I, for one, don't have that issue, and if divination says I can go for it and it sits well with my spirit, then I'm gonna do the work! You know why? I am responsible for every single job I do, and I promise I am not gonna do anything Spirit tells me not to do. I'm too experienced for that. When I was young, I got my butt spanked by Spirit for not listening. Like my mama used to say, "A hard head makes a soft behind!"

This work has never been about playing nice or being sugary and sweet. The ancestors who began working Conjure couldn't afford to be. These folks were enslaved and their lives depended on them knowing what to do to protect their families in a time when just looking wrong could get you killed. You have to get out of the twenty-first-century mindset and go way back to a time when folks thought it was okay to own another human and treat them any kind of way. We have something today that the ancestors didn't have, and that is the freedom to either do or not do something. So if these works are not for you, that's fine. We each decide what we will and will not do. I just want to give y'all a heads-up this is a little different than my normal writings. Peace, be still!

Although I have written about love, domination, controlling, and such in other places, this book will be a little different. This time I'm going to add some old works. These are works that I learned when I was young. I have never written about them and have only taught them to a few. But as I get older, I feel like they need to be recorded so they will not be lost.

Yes, this book is gonna have works in it dealing with animal parts. This is the real ole-school work. These are works that many nowadays don't know, don't work with anymore, or just don't teach.

If you want to understand this type of magic, you should have an understanding of our ancestors who practiced it. It may seem too simple to seem real, but you have to understand, the ancestors were simple, down-to-earth people. They worked from daylight until dark; by the time the end of the day came they were too tired to do an elaborate ritual. The work was practiced in their everyday life from the way they swept their yards to the way they threw out old dishwater. So please don't be fooled by the simplicity of this type of work—it holds the power of thousands of ancestors behind it.

There have been many a disagreement about Christianity in Conjure. Some will argue that the ancestors were not Christian, and others will claim they were. I feel both sides have part of the story right. We have to look at what we know and use our common sense to understand the whole picture.

Let's look at what we all agree on: Slavers went to the African continent, and there they stole the ancestors from their homes to sell them into bondage! This is fact, and there's no denying it. It's also fact that they split up families and not all the ancestors spoke the same language and they didn't come from the same tribes and nations. They were placed in the hull of the ships, chained together like sardines in a can! Another fact is they were left in the hull of these ships with no windows for air—the dead and the living alike.

The ancestors were a powerful people—otherwise how in the world could they survive all of those horrors just to get to a world they knew nothing about? Then when they finally were brought up out of the depths of hell, they were treated no better than a dog or a wild animal! Once they were off the ship, they were usually put in cages to wait for their turn on the auction block where they were humiliated by being stripped down with strangers' hands all over them in front of folks they knew nothing about. I cannot even get my head around the pain and humiliation they must have felt.

My knowledge of history and stories that have been passed down from my elders plus my own common sense tell me that the ancestors were forced into Christianity no matter how folks try to paint a different picture. There is no way in hell they would have been allowed to practice their religious beliefs and spirituality as slaves! I was raised in the Deep South and I'm six-and-a-half decades old—I know how it is there, and unless you come from there or you live there, you probably won't understand the culture or the folks that live there.

I'm sure some tried to fight back, but that didn't do any good or help matters. In order to understand, you have to think back to the realities of that dark time of slavery. The ancestors were not allowed to look a white person in the eye much less touch them; they could be beat or put to death for such an offense! So to think that they were not forced into becoming Christian is just ridiculous. Of course, they were forced into it. They couldn't do anything or go anywhere without permission.

Even so, the praise house did become a safe haven for them even if it was forced on them! The ancestors were very tricky and intelligent. They learned to let those ole massas see what they wanted to see! The slave owners thought they ran them, but the ancestors found ways to worship and work their own magic. They couldn't have drums, so they'd stomp their feet and clap their hands. They were not allowed to meet—yet they could gather on Sundays at the praise house. They were not supposed to visit—yet they did so under the guise of prayer in the praise house. I'm sure by the second generation all the ancestors had been forced to become Christians, but I believe that they became the kind of Christian they wanted to be! They knew the Old Testament, and they made it work for them.

Even though they were forced into Christianity, it became a way of life for them. They used the ole spirituals to share messages with each other. They used the chapters and verses in the Old Testament as codes. How can you not respect that? They did what they had to do to survive. They were a powerful, intelligent, tricky group of elders—they had to be. Everything they knew was taken away from them—all they had was their wisdom, dignity, and pride. Folks say Christianity is oppressive, and it is; the ancestors were already oppressed, so they made it work to their advantage.

This work is not the same as what might have come from their homelands—everyone should be able to see that. It's impossible! Conjure came out of slavery, and no matter how much we may wish it weren't so, it is. I have never been one to argue with folks. I always let the facts and folks' common sense clear things up. Christianity has harmed a lot of people, and there is no denying that or changing the facts.

The foundation of this work is the ancestors and the words of power they drew on from the Bible. I say that loud for the folks in the back! The blood of the ancestors flows in the earth we walk on, the earth that the roots, herbs, and plants we work with grow in—especially in the Deep South where slavery was the strongest. The books of the Old Testament hold the words of power we need for our work to become strong and successful.

I refuse to disrespect the thousands of ancestors who were captured and enslaved by removing something *they* added to this work! Every time a chapter and verse is prayed, it's not only the power of your prayer that is invoked but also all those ancestors who prayed it before you! They should only be uplifted and never disrespected. Could you survive the hell they went through?

There is power in the Bible even though it has been changed up over the years. I believe that every time a worker does a work and prays a petition every ancestor who prayed that same prayer hears the call and is drawn to the work. Draw from the thousands that came before you. There is power in numbers—build on that power for success and for a better life!

As a conjure worker, I work with the power of the spirits of place, dirts, minerals of the earth, herbs, roots, and curios—and the chapters and verses in the Bible. It ain't Conjure if you *remove the Bible from it*. To remove the Bible is to white-wash the work, plain and simple.

Still, to be clear, Conjure is not a religion—it is a practice. Most conjure workers are Christians but not all of them. Most workers use prayer in their work, but again some do not. You don't *have to* be Christian to practice Hoodoo. You can have any religious preference you want and still do this work *as long as you keep the Bible in the work*.

Like many other types of folk magic, Hoodoo attributes magical properties to herbs, roots, minerals, animal parts, prayer, petitions, and personal items. Although each generation adds its own twist to the work, the heart of the work remains the same—a living testimony to the beliefs of those who came before us. Hoodoo does not require a lot of elaborate preparation, expensive tools, or specialized knowledge. It also does not demand years of training in order to be successful. The most important tool you need is a strong bond with the ancestors and faith in yourself that your work will be a *success*. Not "I think it will," but "I know it will." Some people view this type of work as nothing more than superstition or the ancient remnants of an unenlightened past. To these folks I say, "Don't knock it until you have tried it."

In modern-day Conjure folks are led to believe that the work is done with roots, herbs, curios, and some dried animal parts. While it's true that you can do works with just these materials, there is more to it than that. Sometimes ole-school workers use animal parts and have since the work was brought over here by the ancestors in the times of slavery—this is authentic ancestral Hoodoo.

To the modern-day conjure worker this may seem gross, but you have to understand back in the times of slavery folks did what they had to do. The works I am sharing are things I learned as a young worker. Times change, but the works stay the same for most ole-school workers. These works are not for everyone—that's as it should be. Being a conjure worker is not always sugary and sweet. Back in the days of the ancestors this work was a necessity. It being a success could literally mean life or death.

Back in the day, the ancestors worked with what they had. Most modern-day city folks can't get their minds around this type of living because in the cities everything is right at hand. They think that even back in the ancestors' time there were mercantiles in every town and surely in every city, but the ancestors didn't benefit from these places—only white folks did! The ancestors were not free to just pick up and go to town—or just walk down the road for that matter—they weren't allowed to leave the land on which they were enslaved! They absolutely had to work with what they had! Animal parts were a big work item back in those days, and they still are with some elders. Like everything else, there was a time to slaughter animals. With the slaughterhouses we have today, I think any time is a good time, but when the ancestors were here, they had certain times of the year to do it. I know from growing up that hogs and such are butchered in cooler weather because in summer chances are they may be full of worms. Small game could be killed at any time for food.

As for my people, when I was growing up in South Carolina, they went to the store on Saturday afternoons. Half a day was spent either in the field, under the barn, or doing chores at home, then after lunch they would go to Lake City to shop at either Piggly Wiggly or Bi-Lo when it came in the late 1960s or '70s. They got everything they needed for the week. At this time most families still slaughtered their own meats.

When you live in the country, almost every part of the animal is utilized; nothing goes to waste. So I'm sure this work wasn't cheap. I'm sure the barter price was high because it was taking food out of the mouths of the family. The ancestors have always been paid for their works. No one works for free—why would they? In modern times we think of payment in the form of money, but money was scarce back in the day: only rich folks had it, so food, roots, and herbs and such were bartered. In order to really understand the ancestors and what they went through, you will have to get out of the modern-day mindset.

When I said this book is gonna be different, I meant it. Also within these pages you will learn works using animal parts. First let me say *no animal should be harmed*: hearts and tongues may be bought at the meat market. Next, I want to remind folks that this work comes out of the time of slavery when the ancestors worked with what they had. Most of the time parts of a slaughtered animal were what they were given to eat, not the prime cuts. There are a lot of works— even cleansing works—where animal parts come into play.

Modern-day hoodoos don't know nothing about it unless they are working with a beef tongue trying to shut someone up or have an elder who has taught them. You ain't gonna find this on the internet. You will have to get out in the communities and find an elder willing to teach you. I'm writing about it here because I feel the work is being watered down and lost by these so-called modern workers. I'm not dogging anybody—I'm just telling the truth: if you want to learn the real work, then hit the streets and find some elders who are willing to teach and share with you!

Most of the information about rootwork has been passed on by word of mouth from one family member to another, or through a worker who didn't mind sharing information. There is not a lot of written information out there except for the work gathered by Mr. Harry M. Hyatt. Hyatt traveled the South talking to conjure workers and gathered thousands of pages of information, although he himself was not a worker— he was a retired minister.

I'm old school, so everything is in my head and in the stories I tell my students so they can retain the work—or what I write about in my books. The ancestors were very smart this way: you can forget a book you read, but you will never forget a good story that touches you in some way. I can remember the first job I was ever taught by my nana to pull someone back working with seeds. Why? Because it was a lesson but not only that—it stuck with me.

God has blessed me to be able to put my words on paper and teach in order to help others learn. There are many other gifted teachers, writers, and workers out there. I've learned how to do the work from family and old folks I've met along the way, along with my own ability to understand the work. There are others who have also been taught by folks they have met or by family members. They may teach or work a little different than I do, but it is basically all the same. It really depends on what area of the South you come from. Methods differ, but the foundation will always be the same.

I'm a conjure woman plain and simple. This is how I was raised and what I live by. I have done conjure work for over forty years. I'm very blessed my mama kept it ole-school when she raised us. She kept our home as close as she could to the culture she grew up in. I'm very grateful for that, even though at times folks thought she was really weird. That never stopped her. She just kept on doing what she was doing. She shared so much wisdom with us growing up, but at the time I thought, "Oh that's just some of Mama's craziness." My mama ate all kinds of food, so it wasn't odd to see her wrap a chicken heart or other animal heart up in white freezer paper and put it away in the freezer! I didn't have a clue it could be worked with until I was in my early twenties—and she isn't the one that taught me this. I learned about saltpeter in my early twenties in my mama's kitchen! She didn't tell me what it was for—she just said, "That's your daddy's medicine," when I asked her what it was. My sister told me, and we had a great laugh over that one.

Conjure/Hoodoo doesn't have a set of rules to follow per se. Conjure workers don't follow a rede, a rule of three, or any of the other New Age stuff that is out there. You are responsible for your own actions. Some folks may feel like it is wrong to do some of these types of works—and that's fine. If you feel it is wrong, then don't do it. We all have to answer for our actions, and we are all responsible for the works we do. I personally don't do works that are not justified or that the spirits that walk with me tell me not to do. I learned this lesson when I was still in my teens and just learning to work. Spirit sees things we cannot see; we don't know what our actions might bring. Always consult Spirit before doing any type of spiritual work. Always remember every action causes a reaction and sometimes the reaction from a work just isn't worth it.

The best way to learn about Conjure and what makes a work justified is to keep an open mind, to read all you can, take some classes and talk with other workers, find a mentor. Don't ever fall into the trap of thinking that one person has all the answers. They don't—myself included. Expect to see folks who work different than you do or how you were taught and who make different choices about what's justified. If we all worked the same, there would be nothing to learn.

A Note on the Structure of This Book

There are some folks for whom this will not be my first book. And others who know something about Conjure. Those folks can jump right into the works if they want to. But if you are new to Conjure or just need some more background, look to the sections between the chapters that can fill you in on the basics.

CALLING A NAME—JUSTIFICATION & REPRISALS

I have written a little about this in some of my other books, but I want to go a little deeper with the subject here since this book will have a lot of what I call hard works in it and also, if we are talking about love, it can be so hard to get clear of our emotions and see what work is needed.

In today's age with the internet and this work being put out all over the place, you have folks trying these practices that really have no business doing it. They have no training and no mentor to guide them in the ethics of the work, and from what I have seen in the era of the internet, they feel they can do whatever they want to and expect to get away with it. They can—until they run up on an ole-school worker like me and some others I know.

People can go into Conjure and get it in their head that folks have it in for them. Or they can do divination or get a reading from someone who may have nothing more than a YouTube video, or read the book that came with their cards as training and think someone is throwing at them. I'm bringing this up because I have seen it over and over again. You would be shocked at how many folks believe they have a family curse or someone has cursed them because of a reader telling them they are—and even going so far as to give them names of people they feel is throwing at the person.

Don't get me wrong, there are gifted readers out there who have trained to do divination and have the foundation to know how to read in a way that doesn't alarm the client and put fear in them. They know what to say and what not to say. Readers that have no training are not blessed with that foundation. I also want to be clear on this: I am in no way, shape, or form saying that folks don't have bloodline issues—they may—or that they can't have a crossed condition or a curse on them—they can. Can an experienced reader help them? Yes, they can—but I doubt they will be giving out names left and right.

What I am saying is be mindful of your actions when it comes to this work because when you are wrong, you become the target of your work.

We have to remember that every action causes a reaction, every hit that is thrown goes somewhere, and if that hit is unjustified and the target is in tune with the spirits that walk with them, they will feel it. Then they will start doing reversals and clearing work. Then what happens is the sender gets hit with their own work; most of the time it is stronger than what they sent because the target is calling for justice as the original hit was unjust.

Remember the work is gonna go right back where it came from. If you have or do a reading and it shows you are being hit and the reader calls names or you jump to conclusions yourself, don't just start throwing at that person. Be smart about it: pray on it and petition your spirits to guide you. Sometimes you don't have to do anything—Spirit takes care of it for you. Just please look at every angle before you jump in.

This is just my opinion, but I feel that folks don't take this work seriously because it seems so simple. Please don't be fooled. In the hands of a seasoned worker this work can be deadly. Everybody and their mama is throwing roots nowadays. This work is no game, and folks really need to think, pray, and do divination before they even consider throwing at someone, much less calling a target's name. Even if you know for a fact—if you caught someone throwing at you—you still shouldn't call their name out!

Even if you have them pegged, you don't know if they are the only ones working on you. Perhaps that person got help. If you call their name and reverse on them—fine—but the work will just continue hidden from your eyes through the others. Like my daughter always says, "You have to be smarter than the average Joe!" You have to remember where this work comes from and how it came to be here. You also have to remember not everyone is like you; there are a lot of shady folks out there.

You may be wondering how exactly you can do the work without calling out the target's name? No worries—I am gonna tell you how. Most folks, when they are told that someone is throwing at them, get upset and fearful. When we do this, we draw that type of energy to us. As a young worker, I often heard from my elders "plant the seed, the tree will grow"—meaning that once the client hears that someone is working on them, it just grows and grows. If they haven't been thrown at, they will still pull that type of energy to themselves by focusing on the fact that they were told someone was working on them in a reading.

It is better to remove that anxiety instead—and that can go for when your emotions run away with you about a love interest too.

So the very first thing that needs to be done is a cleansing to clear away the fear and shift the focus away from the idea that someone is throwing at them—dig the seed up, so to say. I would suggest doing a brush-down with a white stick candle, and petition your guardian angel to remove whatever is there and for them to draw in clarity and give you protection against this threat. Make sure to cleanse the head well as that is where our spirit sits. You should just sit quietly and watch the flame of the candle burning. Take three deep breaths and let them out slowly to clear the spirit and bring in clarity. You should start to feel more relaxed and be able to focus; you should be clear-minded.

Let the candle burn completely out, take a nice warm bath, and just relax. Try to keep the reading from coming back into your mind. Get a good night's sleep, for tomorrow the work starts. You will need a space to burn your stick candles on. You can cover the space with a white handkerchief. You need a glass of cool water and something fireproof to burn your candle in. You can either say your own prayer or you can say the prayer for the guardian angel that can be found online. I have always found that a prayer that comes from the heart is the strongest, but some folks are unsure how to pray and find it easier to follow a written prayer.

When you have everything ready, then you can start. I was taught to do this type of work when the hands of the clock are moving downward—start at five or ten minutes after the hour. I personally would not start this until after the noon hour when the sun is starting to go down into the afternoon. You can start it any time, but I was taught that any works to remove something should be done after high noon, which is twelve o'clock straight up and down.

Once you have everything set up, say any prayers you say before you start any work. Take the stick candle and begin to brush yourself off with it while calling on your guardian angel. You can say something like, "I call on my guardian angel. I ask that you remove any crossed conditions, jinxes, hexes, conjure work, or spells off of me and you return them to where they came from. Send the work back where it came, energy for energy. As I light this candle may it burn away whatever is there and return it to the sender. May my spirit be cleansed pure and protected. In the name of God, the Father, God the Son, and God the Holy Spirit! Amen."

Relax and watch the flame burn. You can also petition and pray more as the candle burns. Leave the candle in a firesafe container and let it burn out. The next day take the water from the altar and pour it on the ground, giving thanks to Spirit. Wash the glass out, and add some fresh cool water. Place the water on the altar, and repeat the process from the day before. By this time, you should feel much better and be able to think clearly. Remember to take your three cleansing breaths before you start your work. You will do the same steps on the third day.

On the fourth day you will take any wax that was left over and the glass of water outside. Find the west side of the yard and dig a small hole. Place the leftover wax in the hole and cover it up with the dirt. Then pour the water over the spot. You are leaving them in the west because the west is where the sun goes down; the west is where we place works that are done to remove something or someone from our lives. Then you just forget about it because it is done!

WORKS OF LOVE

*L*ove is a word that should be associated with the feelings of warmth, happiness, and kindness, but this is not always how it is. Sometimes love hurts. Love is a very powerful thing—it can either build you up or tear you down and destroy your self-worth and self-esteem. You will hear some folks say they are unlucky in love, that no one will ever love them! This always saddens me when I hear this; everyone should know what real love is and what it isn't. Although no two people will have the same perception of love, the feeling of being wanted and cared for is the same in all of us, I think.

When we are born, we are innocent and have to depend on someone else to take care of us and to guide us. These people are not always the best. Some of them have their own issues or mental health challenges and can be quite cruel and harmful. It hurts my heart to say I feel this happens more than we realize or want to admit. Then like the adults who claimed they raised them, the children grow up to either mirror the abuse or with no clue of what self-love is. Self-love is the most important part of growing up into adults. When you love yourself, you grow on a strong foundation that can't be broken. It can be shaken—but never broken.

I think one of the most important things that helps lead us back to self-love is to remember that whatever happened had absolutely nothing to do with us. It all gets laid down at the feet of the folks who caused the hurt and pain. It's their issue, not ours—they had the problem and it really had nothing to do with us. Folks grow up from childhood to adulthood thinking if they could have just been better, done better, acted better, everything would have been different. I'm telling you right now there is nothing that could make a hurtful situation different unless the person dishing out the hurt got help.

Yet children grow up carrying this hurt and blaming themselves for something that was out of their control and really had nothing to do with them. I'm no doctor nor do I have a PhD in anything but my life's experience. I was the third child out of six. Life was not always easy, but my mama made sure I always loved myself and knew how strong I was. In order to take your power back, you have to first heal your spirit and admit that whatever went on had nothing to do with you. Then tell yourself daily how you love yourself and how important you are to *you*. Once we understand that, then everything else falls into place. It takes a lot of work, but in the end it is worth it.

Then we grow up and we become young adults. We are all looking for love and just that right person to live our lives with—to be happy with, to have a home with, and sometimes a large family of our own with. If we drag the baggage from the past into our new life, then things will be a struggle. The way we look at ourselves is what we will draw into our lives. If we have doubts about what we deserve and don't deserve, that is what we will pull to us. Spirit always listens and tries to give us what we want. No one can love you like you can love yourself; self-love is a must to live a happy, successful life.

When we start out with the first feelings of love for another person, we feel the joy, the happiness, the sensation that we are unstoppable as long as we are together. But sometimes it doesn't last and something comes creeping in to steal that joy and break our hearts. Folks who know nothing about the spiritual life don't realize that when there is a huge upset and our hearts are hurt, it is important that we do spiritual cleansings and works to get our spirit back in line. If we don't, things are just gonna build, and before you know it, you have a mountain where there should have been a molehill. We will talk more about self-love in the pages to come.

The Love Altar

Every home should have a love altar in it. This altar doesn't have to be grand or eye-catching; it can be just a simple place where photos of the family are gathered. Find a nice spot in your home. This can be for the whole family or just for the two of you. Cover the space with a nice cloth. Then add photos of happy times, things that mean *love* to you. Get a tin can, the kind ranch-style beans come in—not the smaller can, but the larger size. Now you may be wondering, "What in the world am I gonna do with a tin can on my beautiful altar?" Well, I'm gonna tell you.

You will not hear of this on the internet; most new workers don't know about using old cans to burn their candles in. This is true Deep South, Southern-style conjure work. I don't know why it works; it just does. On the outside of the can using a permanent marker, write the things that you want to be gone. Then either paint the can and decorate it or cover it with some nice cloth. Dress it up because it is going to be the centerpiece of your altar.

Get a flat piece of magnet and place it in the bottom of the can, place photos of the family in the can or just a photo of you and your mate. If the photo is of you and your mate, place the photos together so y'all are looking into each other's eyes. Then put them into the can. You need powdered sugar, lovage, Jezebel root, lavender, and Master of the Woods. Mix all the ingredients together and add them to the can. Pray your petition into the can and keep a red vigil burning in the can. This will keep peace and love within the home.

Love Thyself

If you have never had your heart hurt, then you are a very lucky person! I think most of us know what heartache is and have felt it at least once. This could be from childhood trauma, low self-esteem, a breakup, or not feeling like we deserve to be happy and have the things in life that we want. Each time we are hurt, that is one more nail in our spirit that controls our self-esteem, which in turn either makes us try harder or feel like we are unworthy—most of the time it is feeling unworthy. I was once told that you can't write about or help someone spiritually if you have never gone through it yourself. I believe that—how can you understand how it feels if you have never been in those shoes?

This is a hard topic and most folks shy away from it: one should love thyself above all else! I'm not talking about ego or being full of yourself; I'm talking about loving *you*, knowing *you* can do anything, knowing that *you* deserve to have anything in life you want and are willing to work for! I am so grateful for my mama because she taught us at an early age that we can be and have anything that we were willing to work for. She used to tell us, "No one will ever love you like you love you!" When I was young, I don't think that I really understood those words of wisdom as I do today.

My mama's wisdom was a riddle to me until I got older. When I was young, I thought it meant that I should always love myself—and it does to a certain extent. But what is the hidden wisdom? I have contemplated this for a very long time in stages of my life when things have not gone the way I wanted them to and I have been hurt and let down. My mentor Mr. Robert used to always say, "Let me break it down for ya!" When he would tell me that, I knew I was fixing to get some good wisdom or a lesson I wouldn't forget. So now—let me break it down for y'all. When you just look at "no one will ever love you like you love you," it seems like she was saying always love thyself. She may as well have been, but like most elders, she was being a little tricky also.

I have had many, many years to think about this, and I believe I have finally figured it out. No one is ever gonna love me *the way* I love me! No one is gonna ever think as much of you as you do yourself; when we think that they are, we build ourselves up to be hurt! You will always be disappointed! This may sound very harsh. The thing is, it doesn't have to be. We could look at it as the most honest thing we have ever heard and grow from it instead! I have found that when you look at people or situations with open eyes and not for what you want to see, life is easier. There is less hurt and aggravation in our lives. Like everything else the best place to start is with *you*. I was raised to believe that we draw what we are—the way we see ourselves. It's very important that folks think highly of themselves, to really love themselves! Spirit listens to what we think. Spirit will begin to believe that this is what we really want in our life.

It is important that we love ourselves and *know* we are worthy of whatever our dreams may be for our life. Did you know it takes about ninety days to change a thought? So, if it takes ninety days to change a thought, then it takes that same amount of time for Spirit to believe what we think of our-selves. That's just plain common sense. When things happen to us that upset us, we all wallow in our feelings. The problem is that some folks just lay there in them and forget the way out. This brings on all kind of issues, and sometimes it takes a lot of work to pull ourselves out of it. I have learned this from experience! I now have a three-day limit on the time I allow myself to wallow, and I have had this limit for about forty-five years. My husband actually helped me reach this goal. When we first got married, I was a hot mess. He wanted me to be a powerful woman! He helped me get to where I could be that woman! Sometimes I bet he wishes he would have just let me be run-down—lol. But not really—we have a great relationship.

I think one of the issues is we get so dragged down until we don't know how or even where to start to pull ourselves back out. This affects men and women—it's not just women! It's hard when you feel like your soul has just been ripped out! When all you feel is unlovable, when there is no golden ray of light shining bright, or no knight in shining armor there to pick you up! This is the time when you *become* your own shining light, your own knight, your own warrior woman! It is not easy to do, I'll say from experience. It's hard as hell. It will be one of the hardest things you ever do in your life. I have learned to look at mine as lessons that have helped me grow into the woman and worker I am today. It has not always been easy, and sometimes I really didn't think I would make it. But I did, and I am so much better for it.

I thought long and hard about putting this work in this book, but I feel it is well needed as there are some hurts that spiritual cleansing alone doesn't take care of. Then I was just gonna give the work and not really go into detail about the issues that cause folks to get so low down they feel like that is all they deserve. But I thought folks need to know that I have been there myself too. I do understand!

Before I go further into this and get to the work, I just need to say I am not a doctor and I have no PhD, just to be clear! I am a conjure woman and I have learned from elders, ancestors, and living life! With this being said let's move on into the work so the healing can begin. I make no claims whatsoever about this work or any of the other works shared in this book; we are each responsible for our own actions. I am sharing a work that was given to me by an elder and that has helped me. You didn't get the way you are overnight, just like I didn't. I have found it is usually an accumulation of things. Abuse comes in many different forms, and sometimes it is hidden behind the name of love. Any time we are looking to be loved, we open ourselves, but if you love yourself, you have no reason to hunt because you yourself are enough. Loving someone then becomes a bonus, not a must!

When love becomes an extra and not a must-have, it changes the whole chemistry of it, the entire feel of it. You fall in love because of your feeling for the person, not the *need* to be loved! The need to be loved is already fulfilled within yourself, so love becomes something to enjoy and share. It took me a few heartaches to realize this; I've been with my husband forty-one years as of this writing. I want him, I love him with all my heart, he is my best friend, but you know what? I don't have to have him! There is a difference. I would be heartbroken if anything ever happened to us, but it would not bring me low.

I have found that it takes a whole lot of work to put myself first and to love myself like no other. It is hard because we are so used to putting others first. Now is the time to start doing this one little thing for yourself! Everyone in your life will be blessed for it because you will finally be able to be the you you were born and blessed to be!

Any time we make a big change in our lives it takes a lot of work. One of the reasons is we are basically reprogramming the way we think about ourselves and the way we deal with upset in our lives. When we have upsets and hurt in our lives, it throws our spirit off. I have heard this my whole life, and I believe it!

This work takes a few steps since changes and goals have to be worked at in order to achieve a result.

The very first step is to do a set of three spiritual baths.

For each bath you will need three tablespoons of table salt, baking soda, and Epsom salts. (The number 3 is a very powerful number in my world and all of the number 3 variables.) Here is something not everyone knows: Epsom salts take forever to melt in a bath. So an easy way to do it is put all the ingredients in a pot and steep it. This way your bathwater does not get cold before the Epsom salts melt. Pray this verse from the Song of Songs or what some call the Song of Solomon into the bath:

> SONG OF SOLOMON 4 V 7
> You are altogether beautiful, my darling; there is
> no flaw in you.

This is the absolute truth. We are all born with a beautiful spirit and soul even if life sometimes changes us. This should become a mantra for you every morning before your feet hit the floor and your day starts! Remember what I said about it taking somewhere around ninety days to change a thought. This is where the work starts.

Stay in the bath the amount of time that feels right for you. No two people will have the same feeling for this—it is not a one-size-fits-all kind of thing. When you are done, let the bath drain and pat dry. Do this once a day for three days.

When the three baths are finished, you should feel better and your spirit should be lighter. Now it is time for a three-day reversal working with three white stick candles. I have learned from working with candles and making them for about fifty years that the wax is like a magnet and can pull unwanted feelings off. As the candle burns away so does the condition. This is one of the reasons I feel like a reversal is needed on the road to healing—not only for the spirit but also for the heart.

You will need three white stick candles and your voice. Do not dress these candles. You will be working with one candle a day for three days. Begin by saying the prayers that you normally say before you start to do your work; then pick one of the candles up. Start at the crown of your head with the unlit candle and go around your head with the candle opposite the way the hands of the clock go. Then take the unlit candle and set it on the crown of your head while praying that whatever hurt and issues are there be removed. You will know when it is time to move on. Then hold the unlit candle and move it as slowly around your body as you can go in the opposite direction of the hands of the clock while saying your prayer from your heart about what you need help with. Then starting at the crown again with the unlit candle, brush yourself off with the candle going in a downward motion while praying that anything that is not in accord with your spirit be removed!

Then you light the candle and repeat your prayer and petition. Try to say your prayers and petition at least three times over the candle while it burns. The next day you repeat the process and so on until the three candles have been burnt. Nothing is free and in life, and the reason this is called work is that it takes a lot of time if you are gonna do it right. Still, the benefits outweigh the cost in time.

Once the candles are done, you will need to wait three full days until you start the next part of the work of healing the heart. This will give your spirit time to get settled in the new you. This work can't be rushed, so just relax and enjoy. Remember Song of Solomon 4 V 7 and keep using it as your new mantra!

You need to do the candlework and prayer daily even if you don't feel like it. You need to push through! The truth is that when you don't feel like saying it, that is the time you should be pushing to say the prayer all the more.

Healing the Heart

I've never written about this work I am fixing to share here, but I have shared it with some of my students—or my kids as they are to me. There are many different works that can be done with animal parts, but for this one we will be working toward healing a broken heart. I think that this work operates so well because an animal has a life force. No animal is hurt in this healing work; you can buy a heart at the grocery store. You simply have to go to the meat department and ask for one.

I feel like this work needs to be shared; it seems like there are so many broken hearts and folks who just can't seem to get over certain things in their lives. Healing needs to start with ourselves so we can better help others who are in our lives. And it helps us to better understand folks—we are not so judgmental when we are healthy and healed since we can see things more clearly when we aren't in pain.

What you'll need:

Tinfoil

Needle and red cotton thread to sew the heart closed

Your petition written out, a fireproof container, and matches or a lighter to burn it

Lovage root to promote self-love

Lavender to soothe

Jezebel root or High John root, depending on sex

Heal-all

1 beef heart

A sharp knife

5 white stick candles

Your petition will depend on your issue. Just make it plain and straight to the point.

This is gonna be messy, but it is well worth it. Spread out a sheet of tinfoil, shiny side down. (I'm sure in the ole days they used butcher block paper because there was no tinfoil available.) This is not the exact way I learned to do this work, but it is as close as I can get. I learned this work in the late 1970s, and a lot has changed since then! Respect for an elder has gone out the door and the products from then can no longer be found!

When you are doing conjure work, everything has to be prayed over—even the needle and thread! Hold each ingredient up to your mouth, say whatever personal prayers are dearest to your heart and your petition over it; set it to the side. Burn your written petition to ash. Set it aside with your herbs.

Most of the time hearts from the grocery store are cut in half. I haven't seen a whole heart in a long time. Take the heart and wash it off under cool running water, then set it on the tinfoil. You will need a sharp knife to cut a hole in the center of half of the heart. Be careful so that you don't cut all the way through. Remember the heart is a muscle—it's not as easy to cut into as you might think. You need to make the hole large enough for the other ingredients to fit in.

Once you have the hole made, place each ingredient in the hole you made in the heart as you go. Once the heart is loaded, thread your needle and start to sew the heart closed. I can tell you from experience this is not as easy as it sounds. Take your time—there is no rush. On each stitch say your prayer and petition over the heart. Each stitch is a prayer that your heart be healed of all hurt and pain. Push all that pain into each stitch! It's okay to cry; tears cleanse the soul!

Once you have the heart sewn back together, set it down on the tinfoil. Now it is time to place your candles. Take the very first candle and hold it up to your mouth and pray your heart out to it. Then stick it into the heart. Next pray over each of the other candles and place them at the top, bottom, left, and right—because you want to nail this healing down. Light the candles in the order you placed them. Let the candles burn for about fifteen minutes, then put them out. The next day at sunrise light them once again in the same order you laid them out. Do this for three days. On the last day let the candles burn out.

Once the candles have burned out, wrap the heart up. You can either bury it under a plant that you will nurture or put it in the freezer and freeze it to hold on to the power of love you have worked into it. If you bury it beneath a plant, remember you must keep that plant alive for the work to thrive. I also wouldn't tell anyone because if an enemy got to that work, it would be bad. Not all things have to be told—some things need to be kept private!

A Heart on Fire

January 17, 2017, I posted a photo on my Facebook page with the caption "Heart on Fire." What I didn't say was that it was a work to punish someone.

I did this work on the ex-lover of a friend because the target would not leave them alone and kept harassing them. This is not something you go around doing just because you are mad, hurt, or upset over a breakup. These folks had been broken up for years, and the target would just not give it up. When this type of thing happens, and one half of a relationship will not move on, then *that* is the time to do this work.

Now, I decided not to include the work in the photo in this book because I feel like it could get in the wrong hands and be misused. But I am going to give something for the opposite effect—to draw two hearts closer and bring back the love they had in the beginning. This is a work to do for couples. There are times in a relationship when it seems like the love gets dim and the couple gets into a rut. They care about each other, but the fire is gone. They become more best friends than two people with passion between them. This happens to a lot of folks. Life gets in the way. There isn't enough time in the day, and by the evening you are too tired to worry about romance. After a while it becomes a habit, and before you know what is happening, the relationship is in trouble.

This is *not* a work to be done to tie someone to you. This is a work to spark the hearts of two lovers back up to rekindle the love and the heat of the relationship. This work is *not* to make someone love you again or to make them come back to you. Those would be compelling works—a completely different thing. I feel like I need to make myself very clear about this work: this is something to heat the love back up between a couple who want to save their relationship.

To do *this* work you need a photo of the couple when they were first in love, when their hearts were full of each other, when just being together made their hearts sing! For this work you will also need red cotton string, a beef heart, twenty-seven red stick candles (nine per day for a total of three days), lovage root, lavender, self-heal, basil, and a tablespoon of sugar. You will also need a dozen fresh red roses. This work can be done for same-sex relationships too—you just have to decide which one will say which prayer in the verses from the Song of Solomon we will use to reinforce the love a couple feels for each other. There are only eight books in the Song of Solomon, and each one is about love; they are really love songs. When you have all your ingredients and have each considered the wording of your petition to fire up the passion between you, it is time to start the work.

If the beef heart is not already cut in half, then you will need to cut it. It is a muscle, so you need a sharp knife. Most of the time when you pick them up at the grocery store, they come cut in the package. Take it out of the package and wash it with some cool running water. Then set it on a white plate. Mix your roots, herbs, and sugar together, remembering this is teamwork so both of y'all need to participate. Each partner should run their hands through the ingredients while saying their petition. Once the petitions are done, place the photo in the heart. Then each partner will pick up the ingredients and pray over them the part of the Song of Solomon that is their prayer. Then place the ingredients in the heart. Take the red thread and bind the two halves of the heart together while you each say your prayer. One holds the thread and the other one places their hand on top of the one who is holding the thread and wrapping. Make sure to leave some extra thread so you can tie the three knots after the heart is wrapped. For each knot speak of your love for each other.

When the heart is put back together, place it back on the plate. Each of the participants then takes six roses. Each one will break the head off one rose at a time and sprinkle the petals around the heart on the plate while praying their Song of Solomon prayer. That makes six prayers each over the heart. After the prayers you will each take four candles from the set of nine for the first day. Take the candle that is left and hold it together, each person praying their petition over the candle and then setting it at the top of the plate. Take turns saying your prayer over each of the candles that are left. After each turn place the candles around the plate so they are in a circle. A circle is never-ending; nothing gets out and nothing gets in. With all the candles in place, the participants, while holding hands, light each of the candles in the order they were set down. Say your petition over each candle as they are lit.

Once the candles are all lit, hold hands and speak your part of the Song of Solomon over the work. Repeat it three times each, then let the candles burn out. The prayers and candles should be done for three days. Once the work is done, you can bury the heart under a nice, healthy tree.

SONG OF SOLOMON 1 V 8-17

His verses 8-10 and verse 15

8 If you do not know, O most beautiful among
women,

follow in the tracks of the flock,

and pasture your young goats

beside the shepherds' tents.

9 I compare you, my love,

to a mare among Pharaoh's chariots.

10 Your cheeks are lovely with ornaments,

your neck with strings of jewels.

Her verses 12-14 and verses 16-17

12 While the king was on his couch,

my nard gave forth its fragrance.

13 My beloved is to me a sachet of myrrh

that lies between my breasts.

14 My beloved is to me a cluster of henna

blossoms in the vineyards of Engedi.

Him

15 Behold, you are beautiful, my love;

behold, you are beautiful; your eyes are doves.

Her

16 Behold, you are beautiful, my beloved, truly

delightful.

Our couch is green;

17 the beams of our house are cedar;

our rafters are pine.

Sweetening a Tongue

A lot of folks know about working with a beef tongue to shut someone's mouth. A beef tongue can be procured at the local grocery store in most places because folks still eat them. I cook them sometimes for my husband—or if I have a job to do. In our world today some of this seems out of place, but in the world I grew up in this is all normal. We need to remember that up until the time when processed food came on the scene, folks ate what they killed—all the parts that could be eaten. That is how these works came about.

This sweetening work is one that calls for a beef tongue.

Sometimes folks in our lives feel like we can be talked to any kind of way. This could be in a relationship or on the job. No one has the right to speak to another person in a hurtful way or to degrade them. This type of communication is flat-out verbal abuse and should never be allowed. Sometimes it is folks we hold dear who are talking this way, though, and if we don't want to walk away, this work can help—if it is justified. The one thing that is important to remember is that their bad actions have *absolutely nothing* to do with us—they need healing, and the issue sits on them.

But if we decide for our part that we need relief, we have to choose to do the work. This work takes time and can't be rushed, and some folks may feel like it is wrong to do this type of work to influence people this way. And that's fine. If you feel it is wrong, then don't do it. There is always a price for change. We all have to answer for our actions, and we are all responsible for the works we do. Spirit sees things we cannot see, and we don't know what our actions might bring. Always consult Spirit before doing any type of work. Always remember every action causes a reaction and sometimes the reaction from a work just isn't worth it.

You can find a beef tongue at your local grocery. If it is not in the meat department, ask someone. When you get the tongue home, wash it in some cool, running water. When I was growing up, we had well water with a pump to draw the water up, and we would catch the water in a bucket. That is pure water, but today we have running water that comes out of the faucet right in the house. It's important to wash the tongue because you don't know what it might have picked up being packaged.

The first step is naming the tongue and then cleansing it. I was taught that before you do this type of work a cleansing needs to be performed on the target. With the naming the tongue becomes the target. If you don't name the tongue, then it is just a beef tongue—Spirit has to know where to go sit. (I know some folks are gonna say I am giving too much away. I hear it all the time, but if I don't share these works, they will just die away as more elders are passing.)

Any time you do a work on a target the work has to be named for the target, or you are just playing hit-or-miss. As far as I know there isn't much written about this or being taught, but this is one of the first things I was taught. It doesn't matter what type of work it is, Spirit has to know where to go; it has to have a target or it will be hit-or-miss. For the naming I have found that a piece of dirty clothing from the target helps draw in their spirit and a picture of the target helps to focus on the target.

You will need fifteen white stick candles because you will burn five a day for three days. Like I said, this takes work and nothing is free. You have to give your time to do this work.

You will need to leave the work out, so it will need to be somewhere cool and where it will be undisturbed. I use the small ice packs you can get at the store to keep the tongue from spoiling as I do my work.

Consider your petition to sweeten the target's words to you.

When you are ready to start the work, lay out the article of clothing and place the tongue on it. You will need a sharp knife to make a slit in the tongue, place the target's photo in the slit. You also need an iron nail. Using the nail, write the target's name on each of the stick candles. You can dress the candles if you feel drawn to. I don't dress mine because I want my prayers to fill them. Once you have everything ready, it is time to start.

Pick the tongue up gently in both hands, call the target's name out three times over the tongue, then blow three breaths over the tongue and set it back down gently. Place the first stick candle at the top, then the next one at the bottom, then place one to the left and one to the right. The fifth one goes in the slit with the picture. You go left to right in this setup because you are nailing the naming down—you want the work to stick.

Pick up the first candle you set down. Say the target's name over it three times, blow your breath over it three times, and claim that the target and tongue are one. Set the candle back down and light it. Do the same with each of the candles, lighting them as you set them down. When you get to the last candle, say the target's name over it three times, blow your breath over it three times, and claim that the target and tongue are one. Set this candle in the slit you made in the tongue and light it. Try to go back and say your petition over the candles at least three times while they burn before they go out for the day.

Once the candles go out, you can either leave the tongue as it is until the next day when you begin the work again or, if you are worried about it going bad, place ice packs around it to keep it fresh. For the next two days you will repeat the same setup and burn that you did on the first day of the work. Once the last set of candles burn out, you let it rest until the next day. Then it will be time to do the cleansing work.

I was taught to do the cleansing two different ways. I'm gonna share both with you, and you can decide which way works best for you. I have done the work both ways, and they both have turned out well for me. You will need to make a spiritual cleansing wash; the target's tongue has to be cleansed before it can be sweetened—the tongue that was named and claimed as the target, that is, not the tongue in the person's mouth.

For the wash you need three bay leaves, four tablespoons of table salt, and four tablespoons of baking soda. Place a pot of water on a lit stove. When it begins to boil, add your ingredients. Use a wooden spoon and stir it in the direction opposite the hands of a clock three times. On each stir pray that all the bitterness be removed from your target's tongue. Then stir the wash as the hands of the clock go and pray Proverbs 12 V 18 three times over the wash.

> Proverbs 12 V 18
> There is one whose rash words are like sword
>   thrusts, but the tongue of the wise brings
>   healing.

Once you have said the prayers, turn off the heat and cover the wash. Let the wash steep just like you would a cup of tea. Let it get completely cool before you move on to the next step.

What kind of white candle you need will depend on which way you decide to do your cleansing. You are gonna need either a glass-encased white candle or a white stick candle. The flame lights up the darkness. The flame of the candle draws in Spirit, and the fire of the flame pulls in power.

First Way to Cleanse

The first way to work the tongue is the one I like best. Pour the wash in a bowl—try not to use plastic if possible. Pray Proverbs 12 V 18 over the wash three times calling the name of the target out and asking Spirit to cleanse their tongue. Place the tongue on the clothing that belongs to the target, get your white stick candle ready by writing the target's name on it with a nail. Hold the candle up to your mouth and say the target's name over it three times, blow your breath over it three times, and pray the Proverbs 12 V 18 over the candle three times. Set the candle to the side.

Pick up the tongue and wash it off three times with the wash, each time praying Proverbs 12 V 18 over the tongue three times while calling the name of the target out and asking Spirit to cleanse their tongue. Once you have washed the tongue three times, place it back on the cloth and stick the candle in the slit that you made in the beginning. Light the candle and say your prayer and petition over the work. You should say it at least three times before the candle burns out. Repeat the process for a total of three days. Once that is done, then you will be ready to move on to the sweetening of the tongue.

Second Way to Cleanse

When I was first taught this work, I was taught to soak the tongue in the wash for three days instead. I was taught this work when I was nineteen because of something drastic that happened in my life. Those are the times we never forget. Back in the seventies you could go to the church and get a novena candle, and that is the kind of candle I was taught to work with at first. Later on another elder taught me to work with the stick candle.

Pour the wash in a bowl—try not to use plastic if possible. Pray Proverbs 12 V 18 over the wash three times while calling the name of the target out and asking Spirit to cleanse their tongue. Pick up the tongue and repeat the petition and prayer over the tongue three times.

Place the tongue in the wash, and leave it in there for three days. Hold the glass-encased candle up to your mouth and say the target's name over it three times, blow your breath over it three times, and pray the Proverbs 12 V 18 over the candle three times. Set the candle at the top of the bowl and light it. While the candle is burning, you need to say your prayer and petition over it three times. I prefer to leave my glass-encased candles burning, but you can put it out until the next day if that feels safer to you.

Leave the tongue in the wash and repeat the candle-burning process for a total of three days. On the fourth day you can remove the tongue from the wash and set it on the target's clothing.

The Sweetening

Make a wash with lavender to soothe, licorice root to sweeten and dominate, bay leaf for protection. Make the wash just like you would a tea. After the wash begins to boil, add a cup of natural sugar, stir well, and turn the heat off. Let the wash steep covered until it is cooled. Pour the wash in a bowl. Pray Proverbs 12 V 18 over the wash three times calling the name of the target out and asking Spirit to sweeten their spirit and their tongue. Pick up the tongue and repeat the petition and prayer over the tongue three times.

Place the tongue in the wash. You are gonna leave it in the wash for five days. You will also need a blue glass-encased candle. Hold the candle up to your mouth and say the target's name over it three times, blow your breath over it three times, and pray the Proverbs 12 V 18 over the candle three times. Set the candle at the top of the bowl and light it. While the candle is burning, you need to say your prayer and petition over it three times. I leave the candle burning at this point in the work. Make sure to pray over the work at least three times a day for the next five days.

I know this is a lot of work, but change comes with cleansing and work. You have to do the work to bring about the changes you need in life. On the sixth day wrap the tongue in the clothing from the target. There are two ways I have concluded this work. I have buried the tongue under a strong oak tree or in a pot and planted a plant on top of it. I prefer to plant it in a pot because I can continue to feed the tongue a little sugar water every so often and as the plant grows so does the work.

If you would like to bury yours in a pot, make sure you pick a plant that you can grow. I have done this with lavender and rosemary. You have to keep the plant alive. If the plant dies, the work will die off. To prepare the soil you say Proverbs 12 V 18 along with your prayer and petition into the soil as you mix it with your hands. Burn a photo of the target and add the ash to the soil also mixing it well while praying. Take the plant and gently shake the dirt off the roots. Blow three breaths and repeat the Proverbs 12 V 18 along with your prayer and petition into the roots.

Place a little of the soil in the bottom of the pot and set the bundle on top of it then cover the bundle with a little more soil. Now add your plant and cover it with the rest of the soil. Talk to the plant daily, and then every once in a while, give the soil a little sugar water. Tend to this plant with love and care. As the plant grows, so will the target's tongue grow sweeter.

Come to Me

Get a red candle for your lover and a purple one for yourself. Tape a photo of yourself to the purple candle; tape one of your lover to the outside of the red one. Burn the verses below to ash and add them to your lover's candle. Place the candles a few feet apart. Set the candles so the photos are looking at each other. Light the wick of your candle; this is the guiding light to pull your lover to you. Pray the verses below over your lover's candle three times while calling their name. Blow three breaths in the candle, then light the candle and move it toward your candle a little. Do the work daily until the candles are face-to-face, then let the candles burn out.

> SONG OF SOLOMON 2 V 7-11, 16-17
> 7 I adjure you, O daughters of Jerusalem, By the roes, or by the hinds of the field, That ye stir not up, nor awake my love, Until he please.
> 8 The voice of my beloved! behold, he cometh, Leaping upon the mountains, Skipping upon the hills.

9 My beloved is like a roe or a young hart: Behold,
he standeth behind our wall; He looketh in at
the windows; He glanceth through the lattice.

10 My beloved spake, and said unto me, Rise up,
my love, my fair one, and come away.

11 For, lo, the winter is past; The rain is over and
gone;

16 My beloved is mine, and I am his: He feedeth
his flock among the lilies.

17 Until the day be cool, and the shadows flee
away, Turn, my beloved, and be thou like a roe
or a young hart Upon the mountains of Bether.

Come to Me with a Honeycomb

Wrap your petition in a honeycomb along with a piece of
magnet; place it in a jar of syrup along with spikenard, calamus, lavender, Jezebel root, and saffron. You can also add
these ingredients into a jar of pomegranate juice, which you
can find at the grocery. Once you have the jar put together,
shake it daily while praying your petition. Burn a tealight on
the jar daily.

SONG OF SOLOMON 4 V 8-16

8 Come with me from Lebanon, my bride, With
me from Lebanon: Look from the top of
Amana, From the top of Senir and Hermon,
From the lions' dens, From the mountains of
the leopards.

9 Thou hast ravished my heart, my sister, my
bride; Thou hast ravished my heart with one
of thine eyes, With one chain of thy neck.

10 How fair is thy love, my sister, my bride! How
much better is thy love than wine! And the

fragrance of thine oils than all manner of spices!

11 Thy lips, O my bride, drop as the honeycomb: Honey and milk are under thy tongue; And the smell of thy garments is like the smell of Lebanon.

12 A garden shut up is my sister, my bride; A spring shut up, a fountain sealed.

13 Thy shoots are an orchard of pomegranates, with precious fruits; Henna with spikenard plants,

14 Spikenard and saffron, Calamus and cinnamon, with all trees of frankincense; Myrrh and aloes, with all the chief spices.

15 Thou art a fountain of gardens, A well of living waters, And flowing streams from Lebanon.

16 Awake, O north wind; and come, thou south; Blow upon my garden, that the spices thereof may flow out. Let my beloved come into his garden, And eat his precious fruits.

Steps to Success

Change is hard; any type of change comes with a price. To be successful you have to *know* you are successful! It takes a lot of work! The very first step is to change the way you look and feel about yourself. Self-love is a must if you are looking for a successful life. So much goes on in our daily lives: hurt, anger, fear, feelings of being unwanted—even silence can be damaging. All these feelings can and do weigh us down. Sometimes we are our own worst enemy and we close our blessings off. We literally block our own blessings.

All of the negative things that are said to us and all the negative things we think about ourselves build up and before you know it, we are a hot mess. All these things can lead to low self-esteem and even depression. You must learn to love thyself and put thyself first! This takes time and a lot of work, but the rewards outweigh the work. I'm gonna give you a work you can do to help build your personal power.

Take back that which is rightfully yours! We were not born to be powerless, but life sometimes makes us feel that way!

Pick one word that says in a nutshell what you want for yourself. This word will be your mantra until you reach your goal. Then you can pick another word and work on that word until you have reached that goal. This may seem really simple, and it is—but it works. Following your mantra shifts how you think about yourself—slowly but surely. The first word should be *self-love*. This is something a lot of us are missing!

Here's what you do. Write the power word *self-love* on a white stick candle using a nail. Blow three breaths over the candle, then say your personal prayer over the candle three times. Pray 2 Timothy 1 V 7 over the candle three times, then light the candle. Just relax and watch the flame of the candle for a little while.

2 TIMOTHY 1 V 7
For the Spirit God gave us does not make
us timid, but gives us power, love and
self-discipline.

Repeat this work for as long as needed, then move on to the next power word working, still with the 2 Timothy 1 V 7. This little work can be done daily. Sometimes change comes slowly, but if you keep working at it, you can do this! Take your power back and become the person you were born to be and not the one life has turned you into! Like I said before, everything costs something—nothing is free in life. In order to help others you have to be able to help yourself first. This work has always been about making life better for folks, but it all starts with self.

Cleansing work is the next thing that should be done on the road to success. We are around a lot of different people during our day, and we exchange energy with them—even if we are just walking past them. A good cleansing will clear away whatever you may have picked up during your day and help you to feel refreshed. There are as many different ways to do a cleansing as there are workers. You could ask half a dozen workers what cleansing method they prefer, and I can almost guarantee you will get a half a dozen different answers. None of these workers are wrong—it really all depends on what works for you. I'll give you a couple of examples of some of the techniques I use when I do cleansing work to get you going.

You can work with one of them or one of your own as long as you get in the habit of it. You don't want whatever you picked up during your day to mix with your work or mix in your life. You also need to cleanse yourself after you do any type of spiritual work. This is very important. I am often surprised at how many new conjure workers don't know that you should cleanse before and after a work. If you are building any kind of power, then you are drawing things to you. Not all of them will be good to have around.

If I am doing what I call hard work, such as hotfoot work, I am not going to just go about my business without a good cleansing. I was taught any time you do any work you cleanse yourself, even if the work is ongoing. You don't wait until the job is done, which sometimes can take up to twenty-one days, depending on the work. I have worked some jobs as long as a month at a time; I know that in this day and time we all have busy lives, but if we are going to do this type of work, we need to keep ourselves cleansed.

The Coffee Bath

For this bath you need a cup of strong black coffee, four table-spoons of salt, one cap of vinegar, and a bowl of warm water. Mix everything together, and take it to your bathroom. You can pour this in your tub and soak in it, or you can shower, then pour it over your head. While doing this, pray to your higher power that you will be cleansed. It's best to let yourself air-dry, but if you can't, just lightly pat yourself dry. Since you have removed something from yourself, you need to replace it. You can dress yourself with holy oil first, placing the oil on all major pulse points and the bottom of your feet. Then you can come back and dust yourself with protection powder, making sure you dust the bottom of your feet.

You can make your own holy oil by mixing calamus, frank-incense, and a stick of cinnamon in a bottle of olive oil, then praying Psalm 23 into the bottle. Once you pray Psalm 23 into the bottle three times, the oil can then be worked with to dress candles, doors, or anything else you need to dress with a holy oil.

PSALM 23

1 The Lord is my shepherd, I lack nothing.

2 He makes me lie down in green pastures, he
  leads me beside quiet waters,

3 He refreshes my soul. He guides me along the
right paths for his name's sake.

4 Even though I walk through the darkest valley,
I will fear no evil, for you are with me; your rod
and your staff, they comfort me.

5 You prepare a table before me in the presence
of my enemies. You anoint my head with oil;
my cup overflows.

6 Surely your goodness and love will follow me
all the days of my life, and I will dwell in the
house of the Lord forever.

Candle and Salt Cleansing

For this bath you need a small white candle, a tealight will do
or a small white stick candle. You need four tablespoons of
Morton table salt, baking soda, and a couple of drops of Mrs.
Stewart's bluing mixed for your bath. Take your candle and
starting at the crown of your head wipe downward with it,
while praying to your higher power to cleanse you. I do this
three times. Light the candle, pray over your bath, then get in
the bath and try to soak for at least ten minutes. Either air-
dry or lightly pat dry.

Other Options Besides a Bath

I know that some folks think that if they don't take a spiritual
bath then they aren't spiritually cleansed. This is absolutely
not true. There are other ways to cleanse without having to
get into the bathtub. You can brush yourself spiritually clean
with an egg, broom, or chicken foot too. These tools make it
easy to cleanse daily, all you have to do is set up a cleansing
routine. Let me say this one more time: if you don't have time
to do a cleansing bath, here are some other ways to remove

things from you. These tools will remove jinx conditions, crossed conditions, or anything else that may have been put on you or that you've attracted just like a bath will.

The Egg Cleansing

Eggs make a wonderful cleansing tool. Get you an egg, and let it reach room temperature. Wash the egg with holy water, and let the egg air-dry. Once the egg is dry, take a marker and write your birth name three times on the egg. Rub the egg over your body starting at the crown of your head and moving to the bottom of your feet. Make sure you cleanse the bottom of your feet moving from heel to toe. Getting in your bath, sit in the tub, place the egg on your lap, and just relax. Continue with your petition to be cleansed. The egg will pull all the negative energy from you. When you feel ready to get out of the tub, place the egg in a bag and take it to the crossroads and throw it out. I know it has been said that you can bust it upside a tree; well, I can tell you from experience the tree doesn't always soak up what the egg has pulled off. So it's safer to just throw them in the crossroads.

The Chicken Foot

The chicken foot works because chickens are known to scratch up all types of messes. This is a simple but very effective way to cleanse oneself. All you need is a dried chicken foot, and the first verse of Psalm 23.

You start at the top of your head going downward and lightly scratch yourself with the chicken foot. While you are doing this, say the first verse of Psalm 23. Make sure that you do your feet also, going from heel to toe. If you are removing a crossed or jinxed condition, you would do this for nine nights in a row. This may seem like a strange way to cleanse oneself, but I was taught this many years ago. I was twenty-one when I was first shown this and very ill while I was carrying my daughter. The Black lady my family hired to stay with me taught me how to do this. She was a very special person whom I came to love dearly. Though she has passed on, I think of her often. This is old conjure work. It really does work and it works fast. So before you disregard it, just try it and you will see for yourself that it works.

The Broom or Fan

I keep a feather fan hanging by the door of my prayer room. Folks who come here can attest to the fact that before anyone goes in my prayer room/little shop they have to brush themselves off with my fan. This is an easy way to keep things out of your space. It only takes a minute and a prayer. This is also good for the client because it gets their spirit moving around, especially if you are going to be doing a reading for them.

These are just a few ways to cleanse yourself of the things you pick up during the day. If none of these appeal to you, then find something that does and use it. You wouldn't put on dirty clothes to go on a date; neither should you do conjure work without cleansing yourself first.

Protection

I just want to touch on protection. In life you will meet people with a jealous spirit about them or full of negative energy. It doesn't matter how much they have; they don't want others to have. These types of people are the ones we need to stay away from. We need to try to keep them out of our homes. It can be hard if they are also family members. To me those are the worst kind. They don't have to be workers to cause harm. Every action or thought causes a reaction. Thoughts can hold the power to harm. So when they come to visit, they send out all this muck. If you don't clean it out, then it just sits in your home and can generate all kind of problems. There are works you can do to protect your home and keep all the muck out.

I'm going to give you a few I have used over the years.

First, it's good to spiritually cleanse your home at least once a month, starting from the back of the house moving to the front. Pay close attention to the corners of each room— negative energy seems to nest in corners. Just get a sponge mop so you can reach the corners and high places, and use this mop only for your spiritual cleaning. You can use a cap of ammonia, a cap of vinegar, and some holy water in your mop bucket. While you are cleansing your home, call on the Trinity and your ancestors. Once you get the house mopped, you can dress the doors, corners, and windows with olive oil that you have prayed the Psalm 23 over. This will protect the inside of your home.

After you clean your home, you can place items behind your doors and in your windows to stop jinxes, crossed conditions, and the just plain evil of others from entering your home. These things may seem simple, but they are very effective in keeping these unwanted works out of the home. You can place a whole lemon behind each door. The lemon will draw the negative energy into itself. You can place a small bowl of salt with an egg on top of it behind each door. Holy water in a small cup with a camphor square in the water will also keep negative energies from entering your home. If you don't want to use any of those suggestions, you can mix red pepper and salt together, pray the Psalm 23 over the mixture, and sprinkle it under your doormat. Any of these suggestions will work well. If you decide to use the lemon or the egg for protection, you will need to take them to the crossroads and leave them there. They should be changed once a month. The egg will not spoil unless it has pulled a large amount of negative energy from your home.

When you have yourself and your home cleansed, you can make a protection mirror packet for you and your family. You need two mirrors, some red cotton string, five tealights, and a photo of you and your family. Cleanse your mirrors with some cool running water and then let them air-dry. Once they are dry, place the photo of your family on the back side of the mirror, and cover the photo with the back side of the other mirror. Either way you turn the mirror you can see yourself, meaning the mirror side is facing outward on both sides. This will deflect any crossed conditions or jinxes that might be sent your way. They will hit the mirror and be sent back—as in "return to sender."

In the book of Job 1 V 10 we see that God put a hedge around Job that not even Satan could get through.

> JOB 1 V 10
> Hast not thou made an hedge about him, and
> about his house, and about all that he hath on
> every side? thou hast blessed the work of his
> hands, and his substance is increased in the
> land.

Take your red cotton string and start wrapping it around the mirror packet. While you are wrapping the mirror packet, pray and petition God to put a protection hedge around you and your family that not even Satan can destroy—just like he did for Job and his family. Once you have the packet wrapped, place your tealights around the packet and again petition God for his protection. After the tealights burn out, then you need to place your packet in a safe place. Once a month take your packet out and refresh it by praying over it again and burning another set of tealights over it. This will keep the packet strong and working.

We have talked about protecting the inside of the home and the folks that live there. But what about the outside of our homes? I'm not going to go into great detail about this, because this book is about other works. I'm just going to give you a few ideas. You can make protection hands to protect your property. To make these hands, you need four Saint Michael holy cards, sharp items, some protection herbs or you can use red pepper/salt; you also need four pieces of red flannel. Lay your flannel out on the table and call on Saint Michael. Ask him to protect your home; place one card on each cloth, then the sharp items, then the herbs. Sew each up while talking to Saint Michael. (For more, see Conjure Hands on p. 139.)

Once you have protection hands made, you plant one in each corner of your property while petitioning Saint Michael to protect your home. You go clockwise around the perimeter of the property. Once you have your hands planted, you can go back and sprinkle red pepper mixed with salt. Then once a month go to each corner and call on Saint Michael asking him to continue protecting your home. At these times you can sprinkle either protection powder or more of the red pepper and salt mix. If you don't want to use the flannel, you can place all the ingredients into four small jars and bury the jars at the four corners of your property.

You have to remember, protection of your hearth and home is just as important as cleansing is. I don't think many folks keep up with either until they get spiritually hit. Keep yourself and your home protected.

HOW TO WRITE A PETITION

Petitions are an important part of this work. We have to remember that *words hold power!* When we speak out loud, we blow out our breath, which is part of our life force. That life force, that breath, adds power to our work. A petition can be spoken or written—it all depends on the worker. Our handwriting also holds part of our spirit; it is also a part of us!

When you do any type of work, you have to use your common sense—something some folks are missing nowadays. Please don't let the easiness fool you: this work is very powerful. The best way to learn this work is always gonna be hands on, but that isn't always simple; it's hard to find real elders nowadays. So the next best thing is to read as much as possible and to discern what Spirit is telling you. I'm not here to tell anyone what is right or wrong for them; I am simply trying to share the knowledge that I have learned over the years from my mama and my elders.

Petitions are prayed over or placed in conjure bags, candles, and sweetening jars—just about anything you will be working on. It is important that you know how to write a petition or speak one so it flows. Always make sure your petition is clear and to the point. I can't stress enough how important this is. You don't want the spirits to be confused when they are trying to help you succeed in your work. Too many words can get in the way. Your higher power will bring you what you are asking for—it does not matter if it is good for you or not.

You have to remember you are asking for something and Spirit *will* bring it to you. So when you are making a request and praying for it to happen, use common sense. Be careful of what you are asking for, and make yourself *very clear* on what it is you want to bring into your life. Sometimes things are easy to get into and hard to get out of. So it's better to be safe than sorry. I've written about this before, but I will again and again because I can't stress enough how much power words hold and how spirit will do its best to give us exactly what we are asking for.

Here is an example of what I am talking about.

Let's say I need a job. So I decide to do some work to help me find a job. If I write my petition out and state, "I want a job" or "I want a job doing whatever," then I'll get just that: a job, any job. Spirit will bring me a job, and I may hate that job and not get along with my coworkers or my boss. Also, Spirit could bring a job doing just about anything. You have to be mindful of the way you word the petition or prayer. You have to be very clear on what it is you are trying to draw or remove. What if I change the wording of the petition? Let's try the petition another way and see how that goes.

Date _____

Birth _____

Name _____

I want a job doing _____. I want to make more than enough money to make ends meet (or you can place the amount of pay you want here). I want to be comfortable with my new boss and the people I work with. I want to be seen as a favorable asset to the company. I want a raise within *X* amount of time. I want this to be the perfect job for me.

Signed _____

As you can see from the example, you are telling Spirit exactly what you are looking for from your new job. You want a job that you are good at and will be able to be promoted in. You are asking for a boss that you are compatible with; you want to work in peace and be good at what you do. Before I write out my petition, I will sit down and think of what exactly it is I want to achieve. I may write it out three or four times before I get the wording right.

When I write out my petition or prayer, I always date and sign it to indicate that it is akin to a binding contract.

I'm going to give one more example that goes into our topic of love.

Let us say you want to bring a new love into your life. You are ready to find someone you can live with and be happy with. Find a quiet spot and sit down, relax, and clear your mind. Then write out your petition. "I want someone to love me. I want him to be crazy about me. He will not be able to live without me. I want him to worship me; he will never look at another woman." Sounds perfect, right? What could be more perfect than a guy like this? Wrong! This guy would drive you crazy; he would suffocate the life out of you. He would be so worried about what you are doing during the day he might not even work. He might even become abusive. Why? Because he is so crazy about you.

You have to truly consider the words you use when you are doing this type of work because Spirit will try to bring you just what you are asking for. You might enjoy the attention from the guy in this petition at first, but after a while it would become very old. Do you see what I am getting at? What if we wrote the petition this way?

Date _____

Birth _____

Name _____

I want a new mate brought into my life. Someone I am compatible with, who is loving, caring, and kind. Someone I can find true happiness with. Someone who is a good listener and will be interested in what I have to say. Bring me someone who will be a good provider, who will love, honor, and cherish me. Someone who will be supportive in whatever I may choose to do. Bring me someone I can live my life out with in peace and happiness.

Signed _____

Do you see the difference? You have achieved the same thing in both petitions. Only the second one will get you so much more. Just take your time when you are writing out your petition. Think before you leap. Make sure you know exactly what it is you are trying to achieve.

It may seem like a lot of work, but the benefits are well worth the effort. You have to remember Spirit and our ancestors will try to bring us what we ask for.

I want you to think before you write out your petition. When you take your time and think about what it really is you want to bring into your life, then you can have a happy, prosperous life. But I'm not gonna preach or try to change the way you look at your life or the things you think you need to be happy. This is just some sage advice. Like the ole folks say: "You better watch what you wish for because you just might get it!" Everything that shimmers ain't gold, nor is all love good love! In my line of work money and love seem to be the main focus on most folks' minds. Yes we all need money, and life is so much better when we have true love, but peace and happiness should come first. One more bit of advice and I'm done with this.

I grew up with my mama telling me this and I have had many elders tell me the same thing: What is meant for you will be yours! You always have the choice of how you go about getting it. Be wise. Also if you have to fight for something and there is constant turmoil and upset to keep it, that is probably not for you! I'm not saying that everything will be easy in life that would be a lie, just please be wise in the battles you choose to fight; make sure they are worth it and that they are meant for you to fight.

Now that you understand petitions, you should also know there are some works that should not ever have a written petition or the petition spoken over it where your life's breath could be caught up in the work. That type of work is any crossing works or dark works. Some may disagree with me and I'm cool with that, but let me explain a little further.

We also have to remember that without our life's breath we couldn't live! So why in the world would you add part of yourself to a work that is meant for destruction? The same thing goes for your bodily fluids and will show you what I mean. I have heard of folks bottling up their urine in protection works along with sharp objects and such. That's all good and fine, but what happens when the urine sours? And it will. Then what happens to the work and that bit of your essence inside it?

I have read about this type of work being done. I'm not saying it is right or wrong, but what I will say is my common sense tells me not to do it. To me as a seasoned conjure woman that equals a souring jar. You have soured urine along with nails, broken glass, and other things. I ain't doing none of that.

With that being said, the same thing goes for adding your life force or handwriting holding your spirit to any type of dark work. You could get caught up in the trap you are trying to set for your target. Please be mindful and don't jump into this work with both feet; use your common sense. This work sometimes fools some folks because they think that it is so simple—and it is, but it is also very powerful and can harm as well as help.

SOME THOUGHTS ON TYPES OF WORKS

In Conjure there is work that is considered hard work. Some folks think it is wrong to do these types of works because they deal in taking over a target's free will. You have to understand that as long as the work is justified, it is not wrong. There is no rule of three or Rede to govern the worker's actions. It is solely up to the worker how far they will go; they have to justify their own actions. The works I am speaking of are compelling, Do As I Say, domination, control, and bend over work.

To be honest, I don't do much compelling work—I flat out make them do what I want. Even though compelling work is a gentler type of work, you are still using some of the same ingredients as in commanding, controlling, domination, and Do As I Say work like calamus root and licorice root. You can sugar it up and make it sound sweet by using terms like compelling work, but you are still making someone do what they don't want to do. A lot of new folks get confused by all these different labels put on this type of work, but when push comes to shove, it is all the same. The degree of harshness is the only difference—that, and your petition. Any time you see a recipe with calamus, licorice, dirt dauber nest, Master root, and Master of the Woods you are trying to bring your will on something or someone. These are the strongest roots and herbs that can be used for this type of work. They may be added to different recipes, but in the end it all comes back to the same thing: these roots give us the power to have our own way.

I see commanding and Do As I Say as the same type of work, just under different names. When you command someone to do what you want, you are telling them what to do. When you do a Do As I Say work, are you not telling the person what to do? Once again, the ingredients are almost the same in the recipes for this type of work. The petition you pray over the work may be different, but the recipe will contain one or more of the roots and herbs.

Two more names that go for the same work are domination and controlling. If you control something or someone, are you not the dominating party? You say what goes and what doesn't. Well, if you dominate a situation, are you not in control of that situation where you are the top dog? It is the same kind of work, just under a different name. Even if you are trying to control a situation, are you not placing your dominance over the people in said situation to have the outcome you want? Again, common sense tells us this is the same type of work; it also uses the same types of ingredients.

To me the label on the product you work with makes the difference in what the work is called. All of these are traditional conjure labels and can be used for these types of work. I'm just trying to explain to the folks newly coming into Conjure who may be confused about all these different works that share the same goal. I am sure there will be some workers who will read this and have a fit. That's okay with me. You look at all the ingredients of this type of work and decide for yourself. As I was told: the proof is in the mix!

For me, Essence of Bend Over is the strongest work of this type. You are doing exactly what the label says, which is making someone bend over and do your will. The person that the work is being done on loses all their power. You dominate and control them. They don't have a say in it. You can dictate their actions and compel them to do your will. Have you noticed the words I am using to explain what Essence of Bend Over is used for? This is traditional conjure work at its best. If this work is done right, the person you are working on does not have a chance. They are strictly under your command to make them do what you want. Here are two simple ways to use the oil and incense of Essence of Bend Over. Just because these may seem simple do not underestimate them.

You can take the Essence of Bend Over incense and write out a petition with what you want to happen with your target. Step outside and face the east, place the incense on top of your petition and light it. Once the incense and paper have burned, you can bury the ashes in your yard facing east.

Get a bottle of Essence of Bend Over oil. Pour a little out of the bottle so you have room to add your petition and some personal concerns that belong to the person you want to work on. Every day shake the bottle while calling the person's name and stating your petition. When you are going to be around the person, rub a little of the oil on your hands. When you touch them, they come in contact with the work.

Before we get to the work, I just have one more thing I would like to point out. You will notice that all my recipes basically have the same ingredients for this type of work. That is because these roots and herbs are the strongest you can use when doing this type of work. The recipes may vary, but they will all consist of two or more of the roots used for this type of work.

CONTROLLING WORKS

Controlling work is done when you need to get a situation or a target under control. This is what I call a hard work because you are interfering with someone's free will. It may seem extreme, but sometimes this type of work is necessary. I know some folks are against this type of work altogether, but just because you know how to do a work doesn't mean you have to use it. As always, it is up to the worker how far they are willing to go. I'm gonna share with you a few of the ways this work can be achieved. You and you alone are responsible for deciding if this work is needed. Sometimes it is!

Saint Martha for Controlling Work

Some think that controlling work is wrong! I say if the work needs to be done, then do it. What might be wrong for one person may not be for another.

If you ask St. Martha for help for this type of work, you have to be faithful and keep a light burning. You also need to set up an altar. As an offering you can give her coffee with a cross in the container. I always give her the offering *before* she does the work. I have found for myself I get better results by doing it this way. You can work with her however you please, but I have found she likes her offerings first. Now you must light a green candle every Tuesday and let it burn until it burns out. Then on the next Tuesday light another repeating the same request. Sometimes she can be slow in answering your prayers and petitions, but that doesn't mean she won't answer. It may just take a little more time.

It has been my experience that it generally takes about two weeks before you see a big change. But once she gets a hold of the target, they will be caught. I always petition her to dominate and control the target as she does the dragon at her feet. If there is a lot of fussing and angry words being spoken, I ask her to silence them. From my experience she is a powerful warrior when it comes to helping deal with men. She will deal with them with a heavy hand, although I have heard it said that she will also work with some men. If you need her, call on her; she will be there for you. Not all men are bad, but some of them can be really cruel. Saint Martha will set them down.

She is all about the hearth and home. She will make sure your home runs smoothly. She does not help with money per se, but you can petition her to help pay the bills and to keep food on the table. I was taught to never go to her for money except for bills and such. St. Martha not only keeps your home up, but she will also bring back a man who has left you.

Over the years I have done a lot of work with St. Martha, not only for myself but for my clients. St. Martha is not real crazy about men and will work hard and fast on them. This type of work is not suited for everyone; some workers won't touch it. As I tell all of my students, you must always do what is right for you! If you feel a job is wrong, then please don't do it, but for those who truly need this type of work, below is something I have used with great success while petitioning St. Martha.

You must do a consultation before you do any type of work. I do three different styles of divination before I take on this type of work so I know it is justified. I have never been one to jump in with both feet. I always look at a work from every angle and pray on it before I ever start something. You have to be mindful of your actions because you are responsible for them. If you do the wrong thing, that falls on *your* head, not the client's, because it is our job as workers to know the right works.

Bring Him Back

Some men are dogs—plain and simple! I am not bashing all men—some of them are very good—but then you have those who aren't worth a grain of salt. There are times when a man must be made to face his commitments and his responsibilities. Some men think the grass is greener on the other side of the fence. And then the woman is the one stuck paying the bills and taking care of the children. If you find yourself in this type of situation, then the work below will help you get him back home where he belongs.

Before you reach for this work, I wanted to explain why I use tealights instead of taper candles or seven-day vigil candles. Tealights simply burn hotter than either a taper or vigil candles. Because the tealight tin gets so hot as it burns, it heats the work up faster. If you have ever used a tealight, then you know that the tin heats up after the tealight has burned only a few minutes. This makes the petition or jars get hot, so the work heats up faster. I have done my work this way for many years—since I tried a tealight and burned my finger on it—and it has worked well for me.

Things you need:

9 green tealights

9 purple tealights

9 red tealights

Your petition

A St. Martha prayer card or statue

A photo of the person (if you have one)

St. Martha oil

Compelling oil

Domination oil

Get yourself ready to do the job with divinations, cleansings, and all your supplies on hand, and then set up your workspace. Place the photo in front of St. Martha, and then place your petition on top of the photo. Take one of each color of the tealights out of their tin and write the person's name on the wax; then dress each of the tealights with a little of each of the oils. Place the tealights back in their tin holders. Now place the green tealight on top of the person's head in the photo, and then place the purple tealight, then the red one. You should have a triangle.

Light your candles in the order you laid them out and call on St. Martha. This is my call to her—you will not find it in any books or online.

Knock on your altar three times and say:

> Holy Mother Martha, I call on you in my time
>   of need.
> I beseech you, Mother, to come at my call.

State your petition then say:

> Blessed Mother, you have never let me down.
> Please dominate *X* like you did the dragon under
>   your feet.
> I ask you, Mother, to bring him back.
> Mother, make him meek and mild as you did the
>   dragon.
> Draw him back immediately, Mother—don't make
>   me wait another day!
> In the name of God the Father, God the Son, God
>   the Holy Spirit, and St. Martha, Amen.

Pray three Our Fathers, three Apostles' Creeds, and three Hail Marys.

Do this same setup every day for nine days. As I said, I have had very good results with this job. Below you will find the standard St. Martha prayer. Either one given here will work, or you may write one of your own.

St. Martha's Prayer

St. Martha, I resort to thy aid and protection. As proof of my affection and faith, I offer thee this light, which I shall burn every Tuesday. Comfort me in all my difficulties and through great favors thou didst enjoy when the Savior was lodged in thy house, intercede for my family that we be provided for in our necessities. I ask of thee, St. Martha, to overcome all difficulties as you did overcome the dragon which you had at your feet.

The Nature Sack

The nature sack, as some folks call it, also known as a nation sack, is nothing more than a conjure bag that is made to fix a man's nature. This bag is only fixed and carried by women. Some say it should be worn hanging at the waist from a belt, but I have found that it works just fine placed somewhere safe out of his reach. You can either wear it pinned to your underwear, in the girls, or it can be placed between the mattresses if the target lives with you. The basic use of the nation sack is female domination over her man. The nation sack is put together for a woman to hold *one specific man*. The reason I say this is that part of making the bag is to take a red cotton string the length of his penis, then dip it in his semen, and tie nine knots in the string while calling out his name on each knot and tell him what he will do. Then the string is put in the bag for safekeeping.

The nation sack is a very strong trick bag used by women to hold their men. It is also very important that he never find the bag—because it is said should he touch the bag, it will lose all of its power. Once the bag is made, it will need to be fed at least once a month. You can feed the bag a mix of Essence of Bend Over oil and whiskey. I usually make all of my conjure bags out of red flannel, but this is one time I used a different kind of bag. I used a red silk bag with gold dragons on it. I used this bag because the dragon is a symbol of St. Martha the Dominator, who is the saint worked with in dominating an uncontrollable husband or mate.

Here is how I made my bag.

You need three red stick candles/tapers that you have written his name on three times, then dressed with Essence of Bend Over oil, then rolled in calamus root. You need two silver dimes that were made in the year of your birth and his.

These two dimes you will name after each of you. Then you need a High John the Conqueror root that you will name after him. You also need a Queen Elizabeth root that you will name after yourself. You need a red cotton string the length of his penis that has been dipped in his semen. How you get this is up to you. Once you get the string ready, tie nine knots in the string calling his name out on each knot and stating your petition.

Now get your name paper ready. Write his name nine times on the paper and then your name on top of his nine times and the words *Bend Over* written on top of them. Dress the four corners of the paper with Essence of Bend Over oil, and make a cross in the center of the paper. Get a white plate and place it over the name paper, string, coins, and roots. Sprinkle a bit of calamus over all of this. Now take your red candles and fix them to the plate in the shape of a triangle; this represents the Holy Trinity. Pour a bit of Essence of Bend Over oil around the candles and sprinkle a bit of calamus on the oil.

Light the candles starting at the top, the next day the one on the left, the third day the one on the right. By lighting them this way you have nailed your target down. Pray your petition as the candle burns. On the third day after the last candle has burnt out, add all your ingredients to your bag. You can add more personal items to the bag as well. You can also add two magnets that have been named after each of you and bound together with a red cotton thread. Once you have the bag ready, feed the bag a drink of whiskey and Essence of Bend Over oil mix. Then blow three good breaths into the bag and close the bag shut.

Essence of Bend Over Oil

Base oil

Calamus (dominating and controlling)

Dirt dauber nest (dominating, controlling, and confusion)

Master root (to master)

Licorice root (to dominate)

Slippery elm (a small pinch to hide the work)

If you are going to dominate someone, you sure better have a little of the confusion herbs in the oil or they might just figure it out. Don't get too heavy-handed with the slippery elm!

Making a Wax Dollie

You need soft wax, the type of conjure oil you choose to use, and herbs. Just get the wax soft but do not melt the wax. When the wax is soft enough to mold, shape it into a small human figure. I never worry if it looks like a male or female because I stay focused on my petition while making the doll. That is all you do! Once you have the dollie made, you can add your herbs and personal concerns to the dollie. I always place my items in the head of the dollie. It just takes a pinch; you don't have to be heavy-handed with them.

These little dollies can be used for all different kinds of work. Once you have the dollie made, then you need to wake it up. Sprinkle the dollie with holy water using the words below. Sprinkle the dollie on each holy name of the Trinity: God the Father, God the Son, and God the Holy Spirit.

> I baptize you, (person's name), in the Name of
> God the Father, God the Son, and God the
> Holy Spirit. From this moment on you will be
> known as (person's name). Everything you feel
> so will (person's name) feel. Amen.

Controlling Dollie

To the dollie add Jezebel root, Master root, and High John the Conqueror root. Then add whatever you can get that belongs to the target. If you can't get anything personal, then write out a petition paper and burn it to ash. Mix all of the ingredients into the head of the dollie. Now if you are a woman wanting to work on a man, one of the strongest roots you can work with is the Jezebel root. This root has never let me down. Jezebel root is one of my favorite roots, I have used it for years.

I have always had a thing about string and knot; in a lot of my baby pictures show me holding cotton twine. I personally like to tie knots, then add them to my dollies. On each knot you make a *demanding* petition that the target follows your prayer and petition. I also add a small pinch of red pepper to heat up the work. Don't get heavy-handed with the red pepper—it takes very little. Once the dollie is done, I hold it in my hands up close to my mouth, blow three breaths on the doll, and then pray the Ezekiel 25 V 10 over the dollie. Then I talk to the dollie and demand that the target do what I want. Then I work an orange stick candle for the controlling candle.

EZEKIEL 25 V 10
I'm going to turn these cities over to men from
the East, who will dominate you. You will
become their property. As a result, Ammon
will be forgotten as a nation.

Write the target's name on the candle and the word *control* on top of their name. Burn the Ezekiel 25 V 10 to ash, and mix the ash with a little powdered calamus root. Dress the candle in some sweet oil and roll the candle in the mixture. Light the candle and pray your petition and the Ezekiel 25 V 10 over it. Then as the candle burns, every chance you get, pick up the dollie and repeat your petition and the Ezekiel 25 V 10 over it. You will need to do a nine-day set of burns on the dollie. When the last candle burns out, wrap the dollie up in a cloth and place it in a safe place. Then once a month you take the dollie out so you can feed it and so you can rework the doll by praying the Ezekiel 25 V 10 and your petition over the dollie.

You can add some of the roots you used and the ash from the Ezekiel 25 V 10 to make the dollie with to a bottle of whiskey along with a pinch of sugar to sweeten the target. You can bathe the dollie with a little whiskey while you are saying your prayers over it. This way every month you are feeding your work; by doing this your work will continue to be strong. It is real important that you feed the dollie, because if you don't, then it will just die out and lose all the power you filled it with.

If there ever comes a time when you decide you don't need or want the dollie anymore, you can place the dollie in table salt and petition the salt to pull the work off the dollie and make it just plain ole wax again. Then you can burn the wax and destroy the work.

The Wax Dollie

You need to make a small wax dollie. To the dollie add any personal items you have that belong to the target. If you can't get anything personal, then write out their name on paper. These items should be burnt to ash and mixed with the wax. Don't overload the wax—a pinch will be enough. If you have to write out a petition paper, then the target's name is always on the bottom, while your name always covers theirs and is placed on top and the power word *CONTROLLING* written on top of that.

Now if a woman wants to work on a man, one of the strongest roots she can work with is Jezebel root. This root will never let me down. I have used it for years. I also like to tie knots in string and add this to my dollies.

While I am tying the knots, I am *demanding* that the target do as my prayer and petition say he will. Sometimes I will add a small pinch of red pepper to this type of dollie because red pepper is worked with to confuse but will also add a little heat to the work. Don't get heavy-handed with it because it could make the target hotheaded. If you want to control someone, then they need to be a bit confused, so they won't figure out what is going on.

Shape the dollie into a human form, then hold the dollie in your hands and bring it up to your mouth and talk to it. Be very demanding in what you tell it, then lay the dollie on a white handkerchief. Now that the dollie is finished you need four orange stick candles. Write the target's name on each candle and cover their name with the word *CONTROL*. Set the candles around the dollie in the shape of the cross; top to bottom, left to right. Light each candle the way you laid them out. Let them burn a little every day for five days, and on the fifth day let them burn completely out. When the candles are burnt out, wrap the dollie in the handkerchief, and place the dollie upside down against a wall or in a corner. Once a week, take the dollie out and pray your petition over it.

Dollie work is very powerful and also simple.

To Calm a Hothead

There is a work I was taught in my teens to settle someone who is hotheaded down. You make a small wax dollie of the target. Load the head of the dollie with lovage, lavender, and a pinch of sugar. Once you have the dollie made, you will need to place it on a bed of lavender, lovage, and a teaspoon of sugar mixed together. Place a setup of four blue stick candles around the dollie top to bottom, right to left. Pray Isaiah 26 V 3 over the dollie three times, then over each candle as you light them.

> ISAIAH 26 V 3
> You will keep him in perfect peace, whose mind is
> stayed on You, because he trusts in You.

You will need to pray over the setup three times before the candles burn out. Do the work for at least three days, and you should see a difference. Put the dollie up in a safe place after that and work it as needed.

Come to Me

Here is an example of a Come to Me work I have done in the past. Come to Me work would be labeled a compelling job, because when I do this type of work, I'm not only going to bring them to me, I'm also going to dominate them. I have a few different ways I might work this type of job, but this is one way that works well. I prefer to work with wax dollies, but for this I work with a dollie made out of red flannel. The reason I use the flannel is because, in order to draw the dollie to me, I use a fishhook tied to a red cotton string. "Why a fishhook for this work?" you may ask. Well, think about it, when you go fishing, you catch your fish and then you reel it in.

The same idea works with the person the dollie represents. You hook 'em and bring them to you. I make my own dollies, I don't work with store-bought products. When I make a flannel dollie, I stuff it with cotton, which is traditional, or moss. Both cotton and moss absorb, so they are both great for dollie work. If I have a photo of the target, I add it to the dollie along with any personal items of theirs I may have. I also add a lodestone or magnet inside this type of dollie because I want to draw the person I am working on.

For this dollie you will add calamus, licorice root, Master root, Master of the Woods, and a pinch of dirt dauber's nest. You can't beat these five ingredients for domination. I also write out a petition paper and place it inside the dollie. You can also add a piece of High John the Conqueror root to the dollie. High John removes all obstacles out of your way so you can achieve success. You can add any other items you want to your dollie.

I soak the fishhook with the red ribbon in an oil I make that contains High John, calamus, licorice root, dirt dauber nest, and a lodestone before I hook the dollie with the line. While the line is soaking in the oil, I set up my altar. For this type of work, I use a red altar cloth with a gold cloth partially draped over the red cloth. I use the gold cloth because to me it represents fullness and richness. I place fresh flowers on the altar and things that remind me of the target. I use three candles for this type of work. They are set up in a triangle. I use Come to Me, Domination, and Do As I Say candles. Each candle is fixed with personal items, herbs, and the oil. In the center of the triangle I have a large magnet. I use a magnet for this because of its powerful draw. You need to have your candle setup at one side of your altar.

As I said before, when I work, I do more than one thing to accomplish the job. The next thing is to make a sweetening jar. The same ingredients are used for the jar, and then add five fishhooks to the jar. Once the jar is ready, place it in the center of the triangle.

Light the candles one at the time praying your prayer and petition over each one of them three times. Next you need to take your fishhook out of your oil and hook the fishhook in the dollie mouth while making your petition, "As this dollie is hooked so will X be hooked."

Now the dollie goes on the other end of your altar. Each day you will pull the dollie a little closer to the candles while praying your prayers and petition. Make sure to work your setup daily until the dollie gets even with your candle setup. Then pull the dollie into the triangle with the sweetening jar. When I do this type of work, I try to go to my altar at least three times a day once I have the dollie in the center of the candle setup. This is just how I work. Do what works for you. Since no candles really burn for seven days, I usually burn another set of candles once the dollie is inside the candle setup.

There are many ways to do this type of work. This is an example of a simple way that gets the job done. I want to say this, use what you have at home and also change the work up if you have to. Nothing is written in stone. Don't stress yourself out about the ingredients or having the right candles. Use what you got. You can even use a paper dollie if you have to. Too many times I have seen old workers say that it has to be done a certain way or it won't work. I have found this simply not to be true. Conjure work is about using what you have on hand. Yes, it's nice if you can afford all the trappings they sell nowadays, but if you can't, don't let it stop you. Use what you have on hand and *know* that the work will be a success.

Beat They Behinds

There are times when a job is hard to do—this usually happens when there is interference from some outside source, but it can also happen if a target is stubborn. I was taught that when that happens, then you *make* them do whatever it is you are trying to get them to do. To do this job you need a sock from both the target's left foot and also their right foot. Take the sock from the right foot and make a dollie out of it. The doll does not have to be perfect, and it doesn't have to be large. Sew the dollie with red thread, and make sure you leave the head open so the dollie can be stuffed. On each stitch call the target's name out and pray your petition, then pray the Peter 1 5 V 11. When the dollie is made, set it aside.

> PETER 1 5 V 11
> To him glory and dominion for ever and ever.
> Amen.

You will need a cigar, a small amount of whiskey, a photo of the target, calamus root, licorice root, Master of the Woods, and dirt from the front and back door. Mix all the plants and dirts together, then write the Peter 1 5 V 11 across the head of the photo and burn it to ash. Combine the ash when it cools in with the other mixture. You also need some cotton to stuff the dollie with. Cotton is good for doll making because it absorbs so well. Stuff all of the dollie with the cotton except the head; load your mixture into the head of the doll and put a small piece of cotton on top of them. Stitch the head up, and once again on each stitch say your prayer and petition while calling out the target's name. Once you have the dollie sewn, then you need to work it in a candle setup for seven days. You will need four purple glass candles—try to find the real seven-day candles if you can. I know some stores still sell them. Make sure you wipe the glass of the candles off first; you can clean them with a little salt water.

Place the dollie on your workspace. Pick up the first candle, call the target's name out, and say your petition. Then pray the Peter 1 5 V 11 into the wax of the candle. Repeat this with each of the candles as you set them down. The first candle should be set at the top, the next at the bottom, then left to right. You then light the candles in the order you set them down, praying over each one of them once again. You should try to go and pray over them at least three times a day until they burn out. This type of work takes a lot of time and effort, but the success is well worth it.

When the candle setup burns out, then it is time for the next step of the work. Get the left sock you saved and stretch it as open as possible. Place the dollie inside the toe of the sock. Pray the Peter 1 5 V 11 and your petition three times into the sock. Light the cigar and blow three puffs of smoke into the sock so it gets on the dollie, and then drop three good drops of whiskey into the sock. You are feeding the work.

After you feed the work, you need to make a loose knot in the sock close to where the dollie is at the toe. Pray the Peter 1 5 V 11 and your petition over the knot three times in a strong, commanding voice. On the third prayer pull the knot as tight as you can. Now the dollie is ready to work!

This work is called "Beat They Behinds" because that is exactly what you will be doing. I have taught this work to very few, but I felt like it needed to be shared before it is lost. I have never heard of anyone else doing this type of work except from my elders. Take the dollie and go out the back door, then open the front door and throw the dollie into the house! Pick up the dollie and holding the other end of the sock slap the dollie on the door frame of the kitchen door. Slap it three good whacks, and on each slap, tell the target what to do. Do this daily until the target obeys, then put the dollie up until you need to work it again.

To Bring Back a Lover

This is a work that I have used to help others bring back a spouse or lover that has left them. This works really well if you put your all into it. You will need a small glass, springwater, lovage root, rose petals, a lodestone, a red heart, a plate, some honey, a St. Michael candle, a red candle, and a black candle. You will also need paper and pen to write out your petition and a photo of the one you want to come back.

Here are the instructions for each of the steps. I want to say this: if you want something bad enough, you have to work for it! You can't just throw everything together and expect it to do all the work for you. I suggest you set up a nice love altar. Put pictures of yourself and your loved one in happier times on it.

Sprinkle some rose petals on it. Put things that mean love to you on it. This will help you focus and lend energy to the work.

Take the glass and add the springwater, lovage root, rose petals, the lodestone, and the red heart to it. Hold both palms over the glass and pray to your higher power to give this glass power to do the work you need done. Now place the picture of your loved one upside down in the glass with the face facing out. Set the glass on the plate; make a circle of honey and lovage root around the glass.

Now take the red candle, dress it with oil, and then inscribe it with the name of the person you want to bring back with your name on top of theirs. You can write this out three, five, seven, or nine times. Set this candle behind the plate. To the left of this candle you will place the black candle. Then to the right of the candle you will place the St. Michael candle. Say the St. Michael novena and ask St. Michael to defend this work and for his protection.

Now this is important. You have black candle, red, and then your saint candle. Light the red candle first, praying over it in the way that you usually pray, then the saint candle per instruction, and last the black candle. Do nothing to the black candle; leave that candle undressed.

Every day you will *move* the black candle away from the other two, a little each day. This will remove all crossed conditions and past hurt from the situation.

If this is done right, the loved one should be home soon.

To Bring a Man Back Home

I was told a long time ago that you can get whatever it is you need by placing a picture of the Lord in a triangle and then placing the work over the picture. I have had good results with this.

For this work you need a picture of the Lord, a picture of the one you want to bring back, a small glass of water that you have added your oils to, and then place a lodestone and a small piece of pyrite into the glass along with a couple of drops of whiskey. You also need three candles: one Attraction, one Compelling, and one Come to Me candle. If you have personal concerns of the target, you can place them under the glass of water along with your petition.

Once you get everything set up, you need to place the picture of the one you want to come back *upside down* in front of your glass of water. Over this setup you need to read the Lord's Prayer and the 23rd Psalm daily. Below is what your setup should look like.

Come to Me Candle
Lord's Picture
Glass of Water
Upside-down Picture
Compelling Candle   *Attraction Candle*

The Lord's picture on the bottom, then the glass dressed with the Come to Me, Compelling, and Attraction oils, then the upside-down picture of your loved one. Use this setup for nine days.

To Bring a Lover Back with a Mirror

I have used mirrors in my work for many years. The mirror is a wonderful tool. For this work we will be using a mirror to bring back a lover who has gone away. This may seem like a simple little work, but it works really well. The work doesn't have to be complicated in order to be a success.

For this work you need twenty-seven tealights. Now as I stated earlier in this book, I like to use tealights because they get hot fast. In this work you will burn them daily for three days in the shape of a triangle to add power to the work. You also need a mirror, a photo of the one you want to bring back, and a dressed Come to Me candle. You will place your petition under the Come to Me candle, and if you have any personal concerns belonging to the target, you can add a pinch to the candle.

Once you have everything ready, dress your mirror with the Come to Me oil. Use the five spot to dress the mirror. (Five spot = top, bottom, right, left, and then the center.) Set up your tealights in the shape of a triangle, then place your mirror, your photo facing the mirror, and your Come to Me candle in the center of the triangle. Light your candles and say your prayers, then state your petition and read Psalm 23 over your setup daily. Do this for nine days. The setup is below.

Tealight

Mirror

Picture

Come to Me Candle

Tealight   *Tealight*

Repeat this setup daily along with your petition and prayers for nine days.

Medicine Bottle and Jar Conjure

Medicine bottle works and jar works are older than I am, and they are very powerful when they are *worked right*. The more you shake and work the container, the stronger the work becomes. If you just let a work sit there, after awhile it will die out. With a jar or a medicine bottle you shake it up daily and keep the work moving around—which in turn builds power inside of the container.

Medicine bottles have been worked since they came out in the seventeenth century when the bottles were glass. Before plastic medicine bottle came out in the 1940s, medicine was also placed into small white envelopes or wrapped in brown paper with the prescription written on them. The idea behind the medicine bottle is that it cures whatever ails you. The medicine bottle is small enough that a man can carry it in his pocket or a woman can carry it in her girls; then when you are around the target, the bottle can be shook and worked. This is a great way to work because you have your target in sight and could even reach out and touch them while saying your prayers and petition on them. This work is built on being tricky.

Then you have jar conjure or what some workers call bottle spells. These works are nothing more than a work that has been placed in a jar. This is an ole-timey type of work. I've been told witches have been doing this type of thing for protection for centuries. Some folks even call these witches' bottles. There is an old spell that I heard about from a witch friend of mine but I have also seen it posted online where you add your urine into a bottle that is filled with sharp objects like broken glass, nails, and other sharp things. I personally am not adding my urine, blood, or any other personal concerns to a bottle with sharp objects in it. I wonder if folks realize that urine sours over time. So my question is what happens when the urine sours to the person that is in the bottle? My common sense tells me that the soured urine will override any prayers and petitions for protection that might have been said when the bottle was made.

The idea may be that the urine will act the same way that ammonia acts in cleansing and protection works, but my skill as a worker says this is not so because this is a bodily fluid that came from the worker. This can be a dangerous work as far as I am concerned. The way I understand works using urine is that once the urine sours it will sour whatever work it was added to. I could be wrong, but I personally am not gonna test the waters with this type of work when you can do the same work without adding your personal concerns to a container of sharp objects. I have jars similar to this buried at my front door and at each of the corners of my yard.

I'm gonna share how I made them without adding my bodily fluids to them. These seem to work really well. If the land and the house are protected, then so are the folks in that house and who live on that land. Most of the time folks forget about the spirits of place. Every inch of land and every house built on it has spirits that it belongs to. This is why folks think there are some places that are haunted or unlivable: the spirits don't want them there. You have to honor the spirits of place and get along with them in order to live in peace with them. I have lived in the same home for over thirty years; I don't plan on moving. I feel safe here, and most of all I feel like I belong here. I feel like the spirits of this place called me here and made it possible for us to buy the place. It does not matter where you may live, you need to honor the spirits of the place. Then they will protect and guard you. Here is how to make a protection jar. I have them on all four corners and the door, but you can just place one by the front door.

Get your jar and cleanse it with some cool running water then let it air-dry. Then go outside and stand in the center of your yard to pour some libation onto the ground. Call on the spirits of the place and ask them to protect the land, the home, and the folks inside the home. They will let you know they are there. Once you feel them, talk to them and say your prayer and petition. Then you need to gather up a little dirt from the four corners of the property and from the front door. When you have your dirt, go inside and add it to the jar. You will need five white, stick candles plus the page from the Bible with Isaiah 32 V 18. Either make a copy of that page or rip it from the book. Pray the Isaiah 32 V 18 into the jar along with your petition; repeat the prayer three times. Burn the Isaiah 32 V 18 to ash and place it in the jar. You also need another copy to burn to ash to roll your candles in. Dress the candles with olive oil then roll them in the ash while praying the Isaiah 32 V 18 over them along with your petition.

> Isaiah 32 V 18
> My people will abide in a peaceful habitation, in
> secure dwellings, and in quiet resting places.

Fix one of the candles inside the jar; the other four should be placed top to bottom, left to right. Light the candle in the jar and say the prayer three times over it. Then you light the other candles the way you laid them out. Pray the Isaiah 32 V 18 three times over the work before the candles go out. Once the candles go out, place any leftover wax in the jar and seal the jar shut. Shake the jar real hard while saying your prayers. The jar is now ready to bury. Dig a hole on the left side of the stoop and bury the jar.

Remember where you buried it at so you can feed the spot once a month.

Working Jars

It really doesn't matter what names you give your jar works; the ingredients you use in them and the prayers and petitions you say over them are what make the job work. There are many types of these jars that can be used. These jars work really well because of the power that builds in the jar when the jar is worked. The more you work the jar, the more power the jar will have.

You may be wondering what I mean by *working the jar*. Well, once you have the jar put together, wake the jar up by slapping the side of the jar while you are praying your prayer and petition in a loud firm voice. Then shake the jar as hard as you can; on each shake call out the target's name and state your petition.

You say, "I call on the spirit of *X*," then state your petition. Do this three times. This is working the jar. You are shaking up the work instead of just letting it sit there. If you just let this type of work sit around, you will have very slow movement that is a waste of time. If you're gonna do that, why bother to do the work at all? Work the jar to get the job moving in the direction you want it to go. Be firm and bold!

When the jar is ready, set it between three stick candles in the shape of a triangle. The candle at the top belongs to the target; the two candles at the bottom lock the work down. Set the jar in the center, light the candles, then pray your prayer and the petition. I try to go to my altar at least three times a day to work my jar. If I cannot make it three times, I at least try to work the jar once a day. Below you will find a few jar works. Remember these jars are nothing more than works in a container. You can make them for just about any type of thing you need. As I said, the good thing about them is you can stir up the work as you are doing the job.

Controlling Jar

Get a baby food jar, an ole-school parchment paper "brown paper bag," personal items for your target, roots, and herbs. Tear (don't cut!) a square out of the paper bag big enough for you to write your petition on. Write out your petition on the piece of bag. Put the petition paper, personal concerns, and roots and herbs into the jar. Shake the jar really hard three times. Call the target's name three times on each shake while praying your prayer and petition demanding that the target do your will. When I call someone's name like this, I say, "I am calling on the spirit of *X*." I have seen this work within hours of making it.

This list of herbs is the only one I ever use for controlling and domination. They have never let me down.

Jezebel root (for women to use)

Calamus root

Dirt dauber nest (I love this stuff; I have often had my whole family out hunting me some.)

Licorice root

Master root

High John the Conqueror root

Queen Elizabeth root

Master of the Woods

You can use these in combinations of three for the Trinity, four for the crossroads, five for the crossroads and the spirit that sits in their center. This was how I was taught to work; I was a little shocked when I first got on the internet and saw folks saying the numbers four and five really were not worked with in Conjure—that's just not so. I have used these herbs for years and they work, even if you just use a name paper and the herbs. They make the job easy.

To Make Someone Do Your Will

Things needed:

> *Master root*
>
> *Calamus*
>
> *Dirt dauber nest*
>
> *Licorice root*
>
> *Powder sugar*
>
> *A pinch of ginger (to heat it up)*
>
> *Personal items (name on paper, hair, nail clippings, piece of dirty sock, etc.)*
>
> *Small glass jar with a tight lid*

When I say personal items, I mean belonging to target. I personally prefer to work with the target's photo if I can get one—that is how I was taught. But if I can't get one, I will work with whatever I have that belongs to the target. Now if you use a piece of a sock, take a piece on the bottom of the sock in the heel section—you just need a small bit. When creating your name paper, write their name five times, then write your own name over theirs seven times.

Now add all of your items to the jar. I always layer the items I place in my jar. I make a bed of herbs, then place the photo or personal items of the target on top of them. Then I will cover that with more herbs. I have found that tealight candles work well to burn on top of the jar. I write the person's name on the tealight, then dress the candle with a mixture of compelling, domination, and controlling oil mixed together. Then I add to the oil a pinch of each herb and the dirt dauber nest. You then burn the candle on top of the jar. Once the candle burns out, pick up the jar and demand the person do as you say. Once you have your jar ready, then you work the jar and again burn your candle on top of the jar.

Now I like to use tealights for this type of work because for one thing they aren't messy and the other thing is that they heat up the work right away. When you light one on top of the jar, the whole thing gets hot really fast. This doesn't happen with other types of candles. You can do it however you want, though—this is just how I work.

Hotfoot Jar

I started working with jars when doing hotfoot works because I have found once you lay the powder down, it affects everyone that gets in it. I know folks say that as long as you pray the target's name into the powder they are the only one it affects. Well, my hotfoot powder works on anyone who gets in it.

The thing that most workers don't tell you about doing hotfoot work is that it can make the target's spirit unsettled. It can make them roam from place to place unless they get some spiritual work done to remove it. It can basically ruin their lives because they will not be comfortable in their own skin.

So this is one work that you really need to think about long and hard and do more than one divination on before you act. The work should always fit the crime, so to say. You shouldn't do this type of work because someone made you mad or did something you didn't like. This is the type of work that should be done if the target is dangerous or has harmed someone. There are other works that can be done to move someone out that are not as damaging as hotfoot work. You should always think before you act. Some of these works shouldn't be done without justification!

When you find the need to make a hotfoot jar, print out Proverbs 15 V 1.

> PROVERBS 15 V 1
> A soft answer turns away wrath, but a harsh
> word stirs up anger.

Write the target's name on top of it nine times going away from you while you pray the Proverbs 15 V 1. You need to burn this petition paper to ash, then mix the ashes with the hotfoot mixture below. Add all the ingredients to the jar. Be very careful that you don't get the hotfoot mixture on you or spill any in your home! This is very important because you could hotfoot someone or even yourself out of your house. This work is no joke. Once you have the jar made, you can work the jar for a few days. Then take the jar to the river, throw it in the water, and forget about the work. When you get out of your car, start shaking the jar; call the target's name while you pray your petition. Once you have thrown your jar into the water, throw five pennies in the water.

Hotfoot Recipe

Ant mound dirt and ants

Glass jar with a lid

Sulfur

Red pepper

Cornstarch

Dirt dauber nest

Graveyard dirt

I use ants because in the same way the ants want to get out of the jar so will your target want to get away. This is my own personal recipe, and I know for a fact that it works. You need to be careful if you make this to use.

Gather the ants and the dirt and place them in the jar. Close the lid tight and leave the jar closed for about twelve hours. Once the ants are not trying to get out of the jar anymore, add the sulfur and shake the jar until it is mixed well. Now add your red pepper. You should add enough until it has a pink tint to it. Once this is done, shake the jar well again. Now add your base powder of the other ingredients. Shake the jar well. You should have a nice pink powder. Keep the lid on the jar tight to keep dampness out.

A Jar to Bring Peace

For this conjure jar you need a baby food jar, paper, personal items, and the roots and herbs listed here. Put a name paper, personal concerns, and roots into the jar. Shake the jar really hard three times demanding what you want each time. I have seen this jar work within hours of being put together. One time my husband and I had this big fight about his family. I'm talking this went on for about a week. We weren't speaking to each other unless the children were around. Well, I got tired of it and made the jar. He was at work, and before the hour was out, he called me and acted like nothing had happened. I still have that jar, and it still works after all this time and will continue to work as long as I keep shaking it and praying my petition over it. From my experience this jar works really well to bring peace.

This list of herbs is the only one I ever use for controlling and domination. They have never let me down. I have worked with these herbs for years; they seem to work even if all you have is the name paper and the herbs. They make the job easy.

> *Master root*
>
> *Jezebel root (for women to use)*
>
> *Calamus root*
>
> *Dirt dauber nest (I love this stuff; I have often had my whole family out hunting me some.)*
>
> *Licorice root*

I work with these herbs for this jar in threes. You can add a pinch of red pepper to the three herbs for the jar if you want too.

Return to Me Medicine Bottle

Take a photo of your target and write the scripture below over the photo. Place the photo in a medicine bottle along with a strong magnet. Add lovage, rosemary, lavender, Jezebel root, and Master of the Woods along with some powdered sugar. Pray your petition into the bottle and close the lid tightly. Shake the bottle while praying your petition. Repeat this daily and burn a tealight on top of the bottle daily. Keep working the bottle until your target has returned.

> Song of Solomon 6 V 1-3, 13
>
> 1 Whither is thy beloved gone, O thou fairest among women? Whither hath thy beloved turned him, That we may seek him with thee?
>
> 2 My beloved is gone down to his garden, To the beds of spices, To feed in the gardens, and to gather lilies.
>
> 3 I am my beloved's, and my beloved is mine; He feedeth his flock among the lilies,
>
> 13 Return, return, O Shulammite; Return, return, that we may look upon thee. Why will ye look upon the Shulammite, As upon the dance of Mahanaim?

Nail a Spouse Down

There are times when we have to get control of our spouse; if you find yourself in such a situation, you can put them in their place and get control with this medicine bottle work.

Here's what to do. Get an empty medicine bottle, a photo of your spouse, syrup, a nail, Master of the Woods, a dirt dauber nest, Jezebel root, and a copy of Song of Solomon 8.

Take the photo and whisper in their ear, tell them whatever it is you want them to do, also tell them that they are nailed down. Fold the picture to you just one fold, then wrap the Song of Solomon 8 around the photo. You then run the nail long ways through their head and drop them in the medicine bottle. Take a pinch of each one of the herbs and add them to the bottle. Hold the bottle up to your mouth and pray Song of Solomon 8 and your petition into the bottle. Add the syrup to the bottle, close the lid, and shake the bottle while praying the Song of Solomon 8 and your petition.

Light a tealight and place it on top of your bottle. The next day get a cup of hot water and set the medicine bottle unopened in the water. Once the water cools, shake the medicine bottle well while praying your petition; then again burn a tealight on the bottle. Repeat this process until you see your results.

SONG OF SOLOMON 8

1 Oh that thou wert as my brother, That sucked the breasts of my mother! When I should find thee without, I would kiss thee; Yea, and none would despise me.

2 I would lead thee, and bring thee into my mother's house, Who would instruct me; I would cause thee to drink of spiced wine, Of the juice of my pomegranate.

3 His left hand should be under my head, And his right hand should embrace me.

4 I adjure you, O daughters of Jerusalem, That ye stir not up, nor awake my love, Until he please.

5 Who is this that cometh up from the wilderness, Leaning upon her beloved? Under the apple-tree I awakened thee: There thy mother was in travail with thee, There was she in travail that brought thee forth.

6 Set me as a seal upon thy heart, As a seal upon thine arm: For love is strong as death; Jealousy is cruel as Sheol; The flashes thereof are flashes of fire, A very flame of Jehovah.

7 Many waters cannot quench love, Neither can floods drown it: If a man would give all the substance of his house for love, He would utterly be contemned.

8 We have a little sister, And she hath no breasts: What shall we do for our sister In the day when she shall be spoken for?

9 If she be a wall, We will build upon her a turret of silver: And if she be a door, We will enclose her with boards of cedar.

10 I am a wall, and my breasts like the towers thereof Then was I in his eyes as one that found peace.

11 Solomon had a vineyard at Baal-hamon; He let out the vineyard unto keepers; Everyone for the fruit thereof was to bring a thousand pieces of silver.

12 My vineyard, which is mine, is before me: Thou, O Solomon, shalt have the thousand, And those that keep the fruit thereof two hundred.

13 Thou that dwellest in the gardens, The companions hearken for thy voice: Cause me to hear it.

14 Make haste, my beloved, And be thou like to a roe or to a young hart Upon the mountains of spices.

Tying Knots

You would be surprised what a small piece of thread, ribbon, or shoelace can do. This is pure Conjure! It is truly old magic. Knots can be used to tie two people together, tie someone's money up, tie up a man's nature, as they say in Conjure, or even tie up a person who is causing you trouble. The list goes on and on. This was taught to me by my son's Godfather. I guess I was around twenty or twenty-one at the time. He showed me how to tie up a person who was giving me a lot of trouble and trying to work magic on me. I have experimented working with knots since then and have used what worked over and over. We will talk about this first.

Stop Someone Bothering You

If you have someone who is bothering you, then you can stop them by tying knots. You need some cotton string cut to a length long enough to tie nine knots in. You can work with the target's photo or any personal concerns you may have of theirs. If you do not have anything that belongs to the target, don't fret: you can still work this trick on them. Write the target's name five times on a piece of ole-school parchment paper. (Tear the paper. *Never* cut it. Scissors cut magic.) Then make a big black *X* across each name praying Mark 3 V 27 and your petition that they are now unable to cause you problems or bother you anymore.

> MARK 3 V 27
> But no one can enter a strong man's house and
>   plunder his goods, unless he first binds the
>   strong man. Then indeed he may plunder his
>   house.

Be forceful with your prayer and petition. Fold the paper *away* from you until you have it in a small packet. Put a few drops of Confusion Oil that you have prayed Mark 3 V 27 into on the paper, praying that they leave you alone.

Now place your paper in the center of your thread. Call their name three times, pray the Mark 3 V 27, and then tie the first knot. Pull it tight and make your petition. It is important that you use a *forceful* voice while doing this. Do this again on every knot. Once you have the packet done, either place it between two small mirrors shiny sides facing each other or put it in a dark place and leave it there.

To Tie Up Money

Now if someone has really hurt you and caused you problems, you can tie up their money. You need your string and a five-dollar bill from them. The five-dollar bill will be your name paper. Write Matthew 16 V 19 and your petition on the *back* of the bill—you will be putting them up against the wall. On top of the Matthew 16 V 19 and your petition write their name nine times. Now sprinkle it with a light coat of red pepper, sulfur, and salt. If you have some personal items of the target, add this on top of the pepper. Fold the bill away from you. This is important because you don't want to jinx yourself. Now place the packet on your string and call their name three times. Then pray the Matthew 16 V 19 over the paper and make your petition of what you want to happen. Pull the string tight. Do this a total of nine times.

> MATTHEW 16 V 19
> I will give you the keys of the kingdom of heaven,
>   and whatever you bind on earth shall be
>   bound in heaven, and whatever you loose on
>   earth shall be loosed in heaven.

Partner Out of Control

Now if you have a spouse who is out of control, here's something you can work with. I have only had women do this work so far. I don't know if it would work the same if a man tried to do this work on a woman. I am just being honest. You need sperm for this one. I'll leave how you gather it up to you—just make sure it is not mixed with *your* body fluids. Once you have your sperm, soak a piece of red ribbon in it. Let it dry. Call the target's name three times, and tie a knot while praying your petition over the red ribbon. Be forceful. Make nine knots total this same way. Put this in a safe place. When you need to work with it, take it out, call their name, and tell them what you want them to do. This is one I can promise you will work. It has never failed yet. I have given it to many clients to use on husbands who forget they have a wife and children at home. Children deserve better than that out of a father. A man might not want his wife, but the children didn't ask for any of that—they are innocent. Too many children go without due to parents who make the wrong choices.

It even works on men who drink a lot; it just takes a bit more work. By now you should have an idea of how to do this work working with knots. You have to remember that this work was built on working with what you have on hand. The ancestors didn't have money to spend, even a piece of ribbon would have cost them back in the day. Work with what you have on hand.

Nail Your Man Down

Working with nails is a big thing in conjure work. There are all types of works where you use nails to nail down a person or a situation. You can even nail down a job that you are trying to get. There is a lot more to this work than some folks realize. We also have to remember that any work done can be undone if you know what you are doing. Please use discernment before you jump in with both feet. Is there a time when it is justified to nail a man down? Yes, there is, and if the spirits say it's a go, then it's a go!

If you have a man who just will not stay where he belongs (sorry guys), then you need to get yourself enough red thread to tie nine knots. You need to get some of his semen on the thread and let it dry. Once the thread is dry, take a railroad spike and wrap the thread around the railroad spike. On each wrap tie a knot while praying your prayers and your petition. Repeat this until you have nine knots tied.

Once you have your spike ready, take it by the front door stoop and hammer it into the ground. Make your petition that *X* is now nailed down and will stay home where he belongs. Then once a month feed the place where the railroad spike is with sugar water to keep him sweet.

Sock Work to Draw 'Em Back

The first time I did this work was in my late twenties when I was young and cocky. Lucky for me the work was justified. Sometimes we get too full of ourselves, and if you do a work that is unjustified, then you might get your butt spanked by Spirit. I still remember this work and the client. Someone sent a lady to me with a handicapped baby. She needed my help. Before the baby had been born, they knew she had some serious health issues, and my client wanted to do something while there was still time. Her husband demanded something different. She followed him, so they had their beautiful baby girl. Even a healthy child can be stressful to care for with a loving partner to help, but a baby with health issues needs both parents to help take care of their special needs situation. It is a heavy load for just one.

Let us just say, when the going got tough, he tried to get gone. He found a younger girl and decided he would wash his hands of his wife and his daughter. That would be a no-go! In a way I did the work for the client, but I was *determined* it was gonna work for the baby. That baby deserved to have her mama at home with her and not out working in order to be able to feed her. In my mind it was justified.

This is an old work, and you can either work with a dirty left sock of the target or cut the seat out of a dirty pair of their drawers. I have always done it with the left sock, but I was taught either way would work. For this work you need a dirty left sock, Master of the Woods, licorice root, lovage root, lavender, and Queen Elizabeth root. You also need dirt from the front door and dirt from the back door. You need a photo of the target and six white stick candles. You also need Ephesians 5 V 31 either printed out or torn out of the Bible.

Start the work by mixing all the dirts and plants together. Burn the target's photo to ash and add it to the mixture. Then pray Ephesians 5 V 31 over the mixture three times and then burn it to ash and add it to the mix.

EPHESIANS 5 V 31
Therefore a man shall leave his father and
     mother and hold fast to his wife, and the two
     shall become one flesh.

Say your petition over the ingredients while you run your left hand through them. Repeat your petition three times. When you have finished your petition, put the ingredients into the sock. I have been told two ways to do this: you can place the ingredients in the middle of the sock or you can place it in the toe of the sock. When the sock is loaded, you are going to tie a knot in it. Get the knot ready, but don't pull it tight yet. Call the target's name out three times and on the third time pull the knot as tight as you can.

Once you have the sock in a knot, set it aside. You need to write the target's name on each of the stick candles. You will need some olive oil, and you need to burn another copy of the Ephesians 5 V 31 to ash. Dress the candles in the olive oil and hold them one at a time in your hands and pray the Ephesians 5 V 31 over each dressed candle. When they have all been prayed over, roll each one in the ash. You just need to get a little ash on each candle. The candles need to be set down in two straight lines. Start to the left and move to the right with the first row, then do the same with the second row. Make sure there is enough space between the candles to place the sock, also be sure the sock is away from the flame of the candles when they begin to burn down.

When you have the setup ready, light the first candle you laid down, pray the Ephesians 5 V 31 over the candle, then move on to the next candle and say the prayer over it. Repeat the prayer as you light each of the candles. While the candles are burning, you should repeat the prayer over them, calling the target's name out as many times as possible because this is the only candle burn done over this work. Let the candles burn out and let the work rest overnight. When the sun is almost high in the sky, take the sock and go out the back door; walk around the house to the front door. Open the front door and throw the sock into the house. Using your right foot, kick the sock all through the house, then kick it into the bedroom.

Pick the sock up and place it between the mattresses on the target's side of the bed. For the next nine days repeat the work of going around and through the house exactly as you did the first time. You should hear from the target before the nine days are up.

You have to remember that the target has a will too. Sometimes when you are working on a target, it becomes a battle of wills, and you just have to keep pushing and don't give up until you have success. This is not the type of work you can have doubts about when you are doing it. You must *know* the work will work. And you have to look at the whole picture. If the target has moved on with someone else, then that person can also affect the work—because just as hard as you are trying to pull the target away, they are trying to hold on to them. This happened when I was working on the man I told you about. The other woman did not want to let him go. She didn't care that he had a wife and a baby that needed him. I'm still not sure if she really wanted him or his paycheck. He had stopped giving his wife money to help with the baby, and the other woman was getting it all. I ended up having to separate them and send her someone else with no wife or baby that needed them. I blamed him more than I did her. He knew he had a wife and a baby girl that needed him, yet he found a side piece to take care of rather than his baby. I would do this job all over again—only this time I know a lot more tricks—and he would probably get something a little harsher done to him along with bringing him home.

This work is not always cut and dry. You have to have discernment, and you have to learn to look at it from every angle. Sometimes you need to do more than one work to get the job done. That is how I have been taught and that is how I have always worked. Knowledge also comes with experience. I have been a worker for a long time, and I am still learning.

PERSONAL CONCERNS & DIRTY DRAWERS

I have written about personal concerns before, but I have never really gotten into them deep or what you can do with clothes that haven't been washed. I have not seen an in-depth explanation written anywhere either. Dealing with clients on a daily basis, I am now positive that folks really don't understand how important it is to keep your personal concerns under wraps. I don't really think folks know how dangerous it can be if someone gets your personal concerns. I assumed everyone understood how important it is to make sure folks don't take your personal items, but with all the new folks coming into the work I don't think this is the case.

The most important thing is to understand what things can be considered personal concerns. Some of you may already know this. But there are folks who really don't understand how dangerous it can be if they fall into the wrong hands when it comes to this work. Growing up, I really thought my mama was weird at times, but now that I'm older and a worker, I understand why she did some of the strange things she did. She didn't give us an explanation—it was what it was! It seemed normal to us even though my friends also thought it was strange sometimes, and they didn't have the same rules.

I'm going to start with *blood* first. Sorry fellows, this may seem like TMI, but this is a really big thing and I don't think folks realize the repercussions this could have to your whole bloodline. If we cut ourselves, my mama doctored us and then she would burn whatever had our blood on it. Growing up, I thought this was so weird, but it gets even weirder. When we became young women and started our monthly, she burned those too. If we were at school or out somewhere and had to change our pad, we didn't leave it there; we had to wrap it up bring it home and put it in our bathroom trash so Mama could take care of it.

When you are a young girl, this seems really weird because most girls are not taught to do this. At the time it made no sense to me. I thought it was gross. But now I understand there was a method to the madness, a reason she did this. Everyone has heard of a woman putting her menstrual blood in food and feeding it to a would-be lover; Mr. Harry Hyatt even wrote about it. That is the main work you hear about where blood is concerned. It is all over the internet now. This is a secret that should never have been put out for everyone to know, but it is in the world now. So I'm gonna give you a few more that folks don't talk about either because they don't know about it or they choose to keep it a secret. My mama knew exactly what she was doing; she was protecting us. If someone would have gotten our blood, they could have seriously harmed us—but not only us; anyone who shares our blood could have been affected.

Let me repeat that! They could have not only harmed us but *anyone* who shares our blood. You understand, right? Parents, grandparents, brothers, sisters, and so on because we all share the same bloodline! This work is not all sugar and spice and everything nice; that is why it has been kept a secret until the Hyatt books were put on the internet. You have to understand that this work came about out of the necessity to survive by any means possible. You can heal, cross, control, and even kill if you have someone's blood. It can affect the whole family if you are intent on causing harm! You have to remember that once the work is done it is out of your hands and Spirit is gonna hit the weakest link—it's either gonna be you or someone close to you!

So many harmful works can be done with someone's blood. Think about it: Our blood is part of our life force. Without it we can't live. It also connects us to our ancestors—not only our dead kin but also our living kin. So the next time you cut yourself shaving or get menstrual blood on your panties remember, if that blood gets in the wrong hands it could be used to harm you! I'm sure some of you are thinking no one would ever try to do anything to you using your blood! Well, I'm here to tell you that you can't trust folks when it comes to this work. A lot of them have their own agendas. Sometimes it's the ones you trust the most that you gotta watch out for. This work is not called tricks for nothing. Be very mindful of who you put your trust in. You might be surprised at some of the folks you are dealing with.

Next, I want to talk about *hair*, which is another one most folks know about—or think they know about. I really don't think that folks understand how dangerous it can be if someone gets ahold of your hair. When I was growing up, my mama trimmed our hair; I didn't go to a hair salon until after I left home. The lady that cut my hair looked at me crazy when I asked her for my hair. I remember it clearly because I thought everyone took their hair with them. I soon learned that was not the case. No one had ever put scissors to my head except my mama, and I remember being nervous as a cat in a room full of rocking chairs and praying the whole time the lady cut my hair.

It wasn't just the idea of a stranger cutting my hair that bothered me; it was also the idea of someone having scissors at the crown of my head. Most of you don't know that a pair of scissors can cut your luck away and all of your blessings if you let the wrong person around your head with them. Scissors are a dangerous tool in the wrong hands. If someone cut the crown of your head and took that hair, they could sour your whole life—and not only sour it, but make you sick and also block all your good fortune. Think about it: if when we are a newborn and our crown where our soft spot is gets damaged, it can maim us or even kill us. This is where our spirit—our life force—sits until it closes as we get older.

Folks nowadays really don't understand this because the elders are dying off and so is all this information. Folks tell me all the time that I share way too much information in my books, but if I don't share the knowledge, then it is just going to disappear as more elders pass. Folks have a right to be able to protect themselves. I want to talk about the *crown of our head* a little more, then I will continue on with the hair. It is important to protect the crown of your head when you are around a lot of folks; this is why I always have my head covered. Not everyone loves me! Let me give you an example.

Have you ever been at a family gathering or event and gotten a massive headache even though you felt wonderful when you got there? Or been around folks who really don't care for you and your head starts feeling pressure in the crown of your head and then starts hurting? Some folks call this the evil eye while others call it a jinx or a crossed condition because the folks who don't like you are steadily pushing those vibes your way. Their thoughts have to go somewhere, and it is usually our heads that catch it. Folks don't have to work roots to make this happen; they simply have to aim their dislike at you. You don't have to take my word for it: put it to the test the next time you have an event to go to and you know not everyone wants you there.

I wanna share something else before I move on. If you feel someone is trying to work you or has sent you the evil eye, you can simply take a pair of scissors and cut a small amount of hair from the crown of your head. Place the hair in a fireproof dish and burn it! I have never shared this before, but it needs to be told. Then you dress your head with plain ole olive oil that you have prayed Psalm 23 over and into. Our head holds our spirit, so that is where work is sent to cross us up. Cut the work, burn the hair, and add protection. This should be done at night when the hands of the clock are going downward. Afterward you should not go outside until it is daylight.

We have to remember that our hair sits on our head, which houses our brain, which controls everything that is vital for us to live. When we are spiritually attacked, it usually causes confusion, panic attacks, sleeplessness, and other ailments. I have even heard of folks feeling like they are having a heart attack except when they go to the ER no one can find anything wrong. Some folks will even suffer from swelling and severe headaches. Any number of things could go on. You have to keep your head spiritually cleansed and be very careful of who has access to your hair.

When I was growing up, we were taught to never leave our hair outside because the birds could get it and add it to their nest; the elders believed that if this happens, you could become ill with bad headaches, have seizures, or be driven insane. I know folks have heard about this, but did you know that someone can bind you up if they have gotten your hair? Three knots and the right petitions can hold you down. Or did you know that using an iron nail and nailing your hair to a tree will cause all kinds of illnesses if the worker knows the right words to say? It is important to keep all your personal concerns safe, but especially your blood and your hair. These hold your life force, and if they get into the wrong hands, they could cause you a lot of harm. Be very mindful who you trust. I'm not trying to plant the seed of fear—just the seed of caution.

When you do this type of work or are around folks that do, you need to use all your common sense and then some. Some folks may not look at a *picture* as a personal concern, but it is! We have very few photos of my grandma; she just wouldn't allow you to take her picture. When I was in my early teens, I took pictures of everything and anybody who would allow me to take their picture. I was probably around twelve or thirteen. I wanted to take a picture of my grandma in her garden. She had the prettiest flowers I had ever seen. She truly had a green thumb. Right when I was getting ready to snap the photo, she caught me and stopped me.

At first my feelings were hurt until she explained to me what it means to have your picture taken. My grandma believed that every time you have your picture taken, they caught a little of your spirit. When you really think about it, it is true! It has to be true because at the moment the picture is being taken that is exactly what you look like, it captures what you are feeling; it captures your spirit at that moment. In some ways a photo is stronger than hair or blood because it holds a little of your spirit. This is why back in the day a lot of the ancestors didn't like to have their photos taken. They thought they were stealing their souls. I prefer to work with photos even over hair or blood because a photo holds a target's spirit at that moment when it was taken. Y'all better keep an eye on all them photos y'all posting on social media—just some words of wisdom.

For me, and this is just me, *nail clippings* are not a strong link to the target as far as I am concerned. Yes, these are a personal concern, but in order to get the nails the target has to cut them off of their feet or hands. I was taught as a young worker that anything that cuts can cut magic and remove it from a target. So, if I believe this, then I also have to believe that when the nail is cut away from the foot or hand the clippers also cut off the spirit that is attached to them. I hardly ever work with them unless it is in binding work. The nails on the hands can be worked with to bind someone's hands or their feet.

Dirty drawers on the other hand are so much stronger for me than nail clippings.

I get calls from time to time asking me about a work that I don't think many do anymore, and that is burying a pair of dirty drawers in the backyard! Every time I am asked about this work it makes me think of my little brother. He is in his fifties now, but he was traumatized by this one work for life. It really isn't funny, but every time he brings it up, I laugh at him. He shouldn't have been so nosey. He was young; he was probably eleven or twelve when this happened. My mama was a tricky hot mess—we could never get anything by her—and I now believe she worked us to keep us good kids and for us to take care of each other.

Like a lot of men back in the day, my daddy liked to run the streets. He just couldn't keep his behind at home. I had already moved out and had my own children when this happened. My poor brother. I'm just guessing from what he told me that our mama told him what she was doing. He caught her burying a pair of my daddy's dirty drawers at the back of the house where their bedroom was. She was placing them where my daddy's head would have laid. My brother told me when he asked her what she was doing, she said, "Burying your daddy's drawers so he will stay home." Needless to say it worked and kept on working long after she was gone; my daddy tried to move out of that house, but he always came back. To this day my brother keeps an eye on his drawers, and as I am writing this, I can't help but laugh.

This type of work is very old Conjure, it can be done with drawers or socks. It is important that they be dirty because dirty clothes hold our sweat and dead skin off our bodies. These are a very powerful link to our spirits and can be very useful in this type of work. For those who may not know, tying a knot in a sock can bind someone and hold them in place. You are locking them down; I like working with socks because you can load them. Dirty drawers are worked with to not only bind someone but also to knot up their nature. They are worked to nail them down and keep them from cheating and running around. There are a lot of works that can be done using dirty clothes, but you don't hear folks talk about them anymore. I'm going to add a few works about that in this book because I feel like they are being lost. We have to remember the ancestors didn't have a lot of money to spend; they worked with what they had.

WORKING WITH
OIL LAMPS

In the ole days most folks used oil lamps to light their homes. Candles were hard to come by unless people made their own. Most of the time they didn't have enough money for food much less money to spend on candles to do work with. So it only makes sense that they would use these lamps in conjure work. I know I caught my mama doing work this way, and I know what she could do. So I trust my own eyes too. I also work with oil lamps that use olive oil and a cotton wick, and I will give the instructions on those. But first the oil lamps.

I use the liquid candle oil they sell at most large craft stores, not the kerosene lamp oil, which will make the house smell like kerosene. If I am doing a long-term job, I prefer to use the oil lamp instead of candles because the lamp wick can be turned down to a slow steady burn, unlike a candle where you have no control over the wick. You can continue to feed this type of lamp as it burns, and you can also adjust the flame on it. Unlike candles, as long as you keep the lamp full of oil the flame will never be extinguished until you choose to turn it off. I know in days gone by people stopped using this type of lamp because the kerosene smokes so bad and has a bad odor. The liquid candle oil does not have an odor, nor does it smoke when being burnt unless you have the wick too high.

By using this type of work—or magic as some call it—the ingredients are infused into the oil, which makes the work stronger because the oil is burnt off as the wick burns, which means the essence of the roots and herbs are burning too. In some ways an oil lamp is safer to use than candles. For one thing, you don't have to worry about the jar breaking or the candle not burning right because you added too many ingredients to it. Everyone has their own way of working; this is just another way to get a job done.

Domination Lamp

This lamp does a few things. I'll be truthful: I started not to put it in this book. Then I decided that the person who reads this will have to decide whether to use this lamp or not and justify it themselves—just like with all works. I call this a domination lamp, but it also controls the person it is being worked on along with a little confusion. Dirt dauber nest is worked with to control, dominate, and confuse a person. A pinch of red pepper will also confuse a person, but I add it to this lamp to give it a little heat. Take my advice: when I say a pinch, I mean just a pinch. Master root is used just as the name implies—so you will be the master. High John conquers all things that stand in your way. Calamus root dominates, controls, and defeats a person's will.

You will need to get the target's sock and remove a small piece of cloth from the heel of the sock. It needs to be a dirty sock. The reason you work with a dirty article of clothing is that it holds the target's bodily fluids from sweating during the day and it also holds the skin that has shed from the clothes rubbing up against the body with daily wear. If you can't get a sock, then just leave it out of the lamp.

You also need to make a small wax dollie and place a few pieces of calamus root in the head of the dollie. Name the dollie after the target. Then you need to write out your name paper. For this you will write the person's name inside of a circle three times. Once you have everything ready, make a bed of the herbs inside the lamp, then place the heel of their sock, the name paper, and the dollie on top of the herbs. Use the rest of the herbs to cover up the dollie.

When you get the well of the lamp loaded, pour your oil in slowly, so you won't disturb the bed. If this lamp is being worked on someone you love, then you can add a little lovage root and a little powdered sugar to the herbs. Lovage root not only draws in love, but also self-love to the target. The sugar will sweeten up the person. Not everyone who uses this type of work does so just to dominate another person. Sometimes this type of work is the only solution they have to deal with someone close to them. Like my mama used to tell us, "You don't know what goes on behind closed doors," unless you are behind those doors yourself!

In some cases, leaving and moving on may not be an option. They may have no other choice but to stay where they are. So folks do what they have to do in order to live in peace. Say your prayers and the petition, then light the lamp. Work the lamp daily for at least the first seven days, then once a week after that. Use your common sense, and always remember anything that can be done can be undone. If your target is smart enough to do reversal work and you have been unjust in your workings, then look out—'cause you're gonna get hit.

Olive Oil Success Lamp

Here is the instruction on how to make an oil lamp using a can or some other container. Do not use a plastic container for this type of lamp. Nowadays you can find glass wick holders at most craft stores, or you can make one the old way. If you want to make your own wick holder, then you need to cut a round circle out of a thick piece of cardboard. Wrap the cardboard in a thick piece of heavy-duty tinfoil. Use an ice pick to make a hole in the center of the circle so you can run the wick up through the hole. Make sure you leave enough wick to place in the can. I usually cut my wicks for this about a foot long and just let the excess wick sit in the bottom of the container, and I pull it up through the hole as the wick burns off.

Get your container and add these ingredients to it for a success lamp: lovage root to promote love, lavender to bring peace, bay leaf for protection, a magnet to draw, a pinch of dirt from a bank, three small pieces of devil's shoestring bound with red cotton string to hobble the devil. Add a pinch of basil and rosemary for success. Place your photo in the container, then add the magnet and all the other ingredients. Fill the container with olive oil and light the wick.

Say your prayers and petition over the lamp as it burns. Make sure to keep the wick trimmed and the container full of olive oil. These make great lamps.

STICKS, STONES & DISHRAGS—
CONJURE MATERIALS

Back in the day when I was a young worker coming up, we didn't have all the frills and whistles like we do now. You didn't just run to the store and stock up on spiritual supplies like you can now. You were taught to work with what you had, and most of that didn't cost money. Dollies were made from ole rags as were packets and such. No one wasted good material on such things; that material was used to make clothes. Folks just couldn't afford it—if they could, then I doubt they would have had a need to work Conjure. This work has always been about survival! It's not the kind of thing the folks that live in the big house would be doing.

I love working with jars, but that is a more modern work. When I was coming up, jars were used for canning. The same jars were employed over and over every year; they wouldn't have wasted a jar for conjure work. Bowls and cans were mostly used instead. Over the years as this work has been brought into modern times, in some ways it has been so whitewashed until the works I grew up learning are almost null and void. I understand that the work has to evolve—but not to the point that it is now where folks think you can't work unless you have a ton of *things* to work with. For me this is being disrespectful to the ancestors whose bones and blood cover the land. This is their knowledge that is just being thrown away. This is the reason I write: so the knowledge can live on.

"What exactly do you do with sticks, stones, and dishrags?" you might be asking. The answer is a lot. These are some of the first tricks I was taught to lay. That's right, I said *tricks*! Folks know nothing about this type of work nowadays. You never hear about it or read about it—and the reason is that it isn't being taught. I may mention it to my students, but I have never written about it. When I decided to write this book, I decided to share some of the oldest works I have learned. I don't want this work to be lost.

So what exactly can you do with a rock out of someone's yard or driveway? A lot! You can either draw blessings into the yard or you can cross the land up.

Back in the day of the ancestors, they weren't allowed much, but they could walk around the land. No one would think anything of someone picking up a rock or a stone. Back in that day and time, skipping stones was a thing. If you picked up a stone and happened to put it in your pocket, no one batted an eye. If you happened to drop a stone, no one worried about that either. It's just a rock right? But, you can charm a simple rock that you picked up out of a target's driveway. That rock will become the whole work, and if you do the work right, you don't have to do anything else.

You can do the same type of work with a stick you have picked up in a target's yard. Don't break one out of a tree of theirs because that will be a living stick; it has to be one that has fallen off the tree and is dead. You simply work the rock or stick as you would any work. It should be worked three, nine, or twenty-one days depending on what the petition is. Once the work is done, then it depends on what you are trying to do as to when you drop the work off. If you are trying to draw the target, then you drop it off before noon. If you are doing any other type of work, then you would drop it off in the afternoon when the sun is starting to go down. This type of work is no joke: use your common sense. The work will continue to function as long as the rock or stick is left where you put it.

Oh my! What about that ole dishrag? Growing up my mama never let the dishrag out of her sight when company came over. Most of the time the dirty dishrags and hand towels for the kitchen were loaded in the washer and a fresh one was taken out to do the dishes after the company left. My mama never allowed company to do the dishes or help clean up the kitchen—she always did that herself. We didn't even have to wash the dishes. My mama tended to the kitchen herself. She taught us that the kitchen is the heart of the family—it was never to be left dirty, and the dishes had to be done before she would go to bed. Keeping dishrags and hand towels safe goes right along with loaning folks salt or sugar out of your kitchen.

My mama never let anyone borrow salt—period. She would give the change so they could buy their own, instead. She believed, as do I, that to loan salt is to open the door for the devil to step in—because salt protects and, if you give it away, you are giving away your protection. If you give away your protection, then you are just asking for trouble. The same goes for sugar. If you give away your sugar out of your kitchen, which is the heart of the home, then you are giving away all the sweetness and blessings from your home. Folks can use the sugar or salt to cross up your home and your family as they both live in the very heart of your home. You are just opening the door up for them.

If someone steals your dishrag or hand towel out of your kitchen, they can tie a knot in them and bind the family to poverty. The dishrag is not just a cloth for cleaning; it is a cloth that is used to wash the plates, pots, silverware, and glasses that your family uses to eat their meals with. Therefore, it is full of the whole family's DNA. This means that the whole family could be crossed up, or just one member, depending on the reason for stealing the dishrag. Folks nowadays don't know nothing about this type of work. This type of work is hard to break because of the knot, but it can be undone if you have the right worker. Most of the time this type of work is done to cause the whole family issues. It will drain the money right out of a home.

Nowadays folks should be mindful of who they let in their homes and where these visitors are allowed to go within the home. I was taught as a young worker to never tie up a person's money—because without money they can't live. Be mindful that the world is full of would-be conjure workers nowadays.

SEPARATION WORK

W e have talked about bringing someone back to us. But what if for some reason we wanted to separate two people? You would be surprised to know how many people go to workers to have this type of work done. Most workers don't talk about the work they do for others, so folks never know how many jobs like this a worker might do. Not every worker will do this type of work; it really depends on how they themselves feel about this work. It is and has always been the worker's responsibility to decide the work they do. That is why it is so important to do divination before you do any type of spiritual work—Spirit may not want you to interfere.

Still, there are times when separation work is needed. When someone is being harmed by a party of people or a person and the issue cannot be fixed any other way, then separation with Spirit's permission is always the way to go. There are many ways to accomplish this. I am going to give you a few examples of how I do this type of work. As always, do what you feel is right for you. If you are going to separate two people, then you will need to sour their relationship first; then the one that you want to leave needs to have some type of work done on them to make them take that step. Understand there will be some type of blowup that will happen between the two parties to make the separation work. There is no way to sugarcoat this—it is what it is. That is why discernment is so important.

This type of job takes work. You can't just light a few candles and expect everything to be done. I was taught that you need to do more than one work when you do a job. Just doing one thing is not enough to get the job done. Everyone works differently, so I am not saying this is the right way or the only way. I am simply saying this is the way I was taught.

Sometimes this type of work is difficult to do. There are many factors at play for why this type of work fails. I have found that the spirit of the target has a lot to do with the worker's success. If the target's spirit fights the work, then you are going to have to work harder. Some folks just do not want to let go no matter what. I am not saying you can't get the job done; I'm just saying that you will just have to work harder to achieve your goal. I have found when doing this type of work that it is best to fill the dollie's head with black mustard seeds. Black mustard seed is one of the main ingredients in Confusion oil.

If you use black mustard seeds in the head of the dollie, then this will keep the person you are separating confused and they will not fight the work you are doing on them. If the mind is confused, then the spirit of the target will also be confused. This will help make your work a success. I personally like using jars in my work. They hold the power you build in them with your prayers and petitions. They are also easy to keep working. When I say "work the jar," I mean to shake the jar hard while praying your prayer and your petition.

Separation Jar

For this work you will make two wax dollies. These dollies represent the two people you will be separating. Build your wax dollies, then stuff the head of one dollie with black cat hair, black mustard seeds, and a coffin nail that you have written the person's name on. Just stick the coffin nail right through the wax dollie's head. For the next dollie you will add black dog hair to the head along with the other ingredients.

When you get the dollies made, you need to name them. After you name your dollies, you need to place them back-to-back and head-to-feet. This way they cannot see each other or communicate with each other. When you have the dollies in place, wrap them with black thread so they stay in the position you have put them in. Once you get your dollies wrapped, place them in your jar.

To the jar add red pepper, a little milk to sour them, and red wine vinegar. Close the jar tight; you do not want this stuff getting on you as you work the jar. As an extra precaution I place duct tape on the top of the jar, then put it in a large ziplock bag. When I am ready, I burn my tealight on top of the ziplock. I don't remove the jar from the ziplock. I see the ziplock as reinforcing the work by locking it in the bag.

I work the jar for seven days: I shake the jar really hard while saying my prayers and praying my petition. Then I burn the tealight on top of the jar. Once my seven days are up, I place the jar in the freezer to freeze the work. After the job is a success, I take the jar and throw it in running water. There are other ways to do this job, but I have had good success with this work, so I continue to use it. Just remember after this type of work you need to cleanse yourself really well.

To Cause Two People to Fuss and Fight

Get you a small jar and to the jar add any personal concerns you may have for the folks you are working on. If you don't have anything of theirs, then write one name going one way and the other name going the other way on a piece of paper. Place this in the jar. To the jar add a pinch of dog hair and a pinch of cat hair. Then add some dirt from a yard where two dogs have fought. (This dirt is not as hard to find as you might think if you know folks with dogs.) Add some red pepper then top it off with some vinegar.

Once you have the jar closed, shake the jar really hard and call the parties' names and tell them what you want to happen. Then burn a small tealight on top of the jar to heat the work up. Every time you want to cause them to fuss and fight, work the jar. You can keep the jar in a dark place when you are not working it. This may sound simple, but it works.

To Sour a Relationship

This may seem like a simple work, too, but it does the job. If you want to sour a person's relationship with another person for whatever reason, this jar will do the job for you. You need a small jar with a tight lid, milk, red pepper, and a pinch of gunpowder, one lemon, nine needles, your petition paper, personal concerns, nine tealights, duct tape, and a small zip-lock bag.

Gather all your ingredients together. Cut the lemon in half and put red pepper on both sides of the lemon. Write each person's name nine times each on your petition paper—one name going one way and the other person's name going the other way. Place the petition paper between the two halves of lemon then put the lemon back together using the needles. Place one needle going one way and the other needle going the other way. Repeat this process until you have used all of the needles.

Place the lemon in the jar then add all the other ingredients. Once you have everything in the jar, close the lid tight and duct tape the lid. You don't want to get this mess on you, so as another precaution put the jar inside a small ziplock. To wake the jar up, shake it as hard as you can while you pray your petition in a loud, strong voice. Then light a tealight on top of the jar.

Shake the jar then place a candle on the jar for nine days. When the nine days are up, bury the jar in the west. So every time the sun goes down the relationship will sour more.

Stop the Other Woman

Not all women are decent and they don't care if a man belongs to someone else or if he has a family or small children; they will still go after them. I know it takes two to tango and it is not all the woman's fault—the man has to share the responsibility for their actions. I know sometimes men lie and claim they are single, but when the truth comes out, the woman should walk away and leave him alone. Most women don't, though, because they are already in too deep by the time they find out.

If you find yourself in this situation, Proverbs 6 V 24-29 can be worked to stop the other woman from stealing your man. You can nail her down, separate them, and move her out of the way. You will need to get a small glass jar with a tight lid on it. Take her photo and turn her upside down; run a nail through the photo starting at her feet. Keep her head going downward. Place the photo in the jar. To the jar add poppy seeds, red pepper, and black mustard seeds, and then cover all the ingredients with red vinegar. Close the lid tightly.

Take a photo of your man and tape it to the outside of the jar. Work the hell out of the jar daily and burn a tealight on top of the jar. It won't be long until she will have to find herself a new man.

> PROVERBS 6 V 24–29
>
> 24 To keep thee from the evil woman, from the flattery of the tongue of a strange woman.
>
> 25 Lust not after her beauty in thine heart; neither let her take thee with her eyelids.
>
> 26 For by means of a whorish woman [a man is brought] to a piece of bread: and the adulteress will hunt for the precious life.
>
> 27 Can a man take fire in his bosom, and his clothes not be burned?
>
> 28 Can one go upon hot coals, and his feet not be burned?
>
> 29 So he that goeth in to his neighbour's wife; whosoever toucheth her shall not be innocent.

Water Works

I was taught that if you wanted to remove something from you, you threw it in running water. As the water flows, it moves away from you. Common sense tells us this along with what we are taught in school. When the tide moves out, it will take whatever is thrown in the water away with it.

I was in a debate a long time ago about this subject. The whole thing started over a work someone bought from a worker to bring something or someone *to them*. I was taught that to bring something or someone to you, you bury it in your yard facing east or place it by your front door near your front stoop. The sun rises or comes up in the east, so it will bring things to you.

The argument was that with the rise of the river it would bring whatever you needed to you. I disagree 100 percent. Yes, when the river rises, it does bring to you—again common sense tells us this—but common sense also tells us that when the river goes down, it will remove what came when it rose. Then it was said, well, you could make holes in the top of the jar or use a packet, then throw it in and it will move a little ways and sink—common sense also tells us this is right. But my question is, where does this tell us that it will come back to us? If it sinks, it is not going anywhere, not to us or away from us: it will just sit there.

Let's look at another example. This comes out of one of the Hyatt works. I'm just going to give the gist of the work. The work was done to harm someone. The worker makes a packet and places it on a dock with a string to hold it in place. When the water comes up, the person being worked on gets no relief. Why? Because it is bringing the work to them. But when the water goes down, the work goes away for a while until the water rises again and the work is brought back upon the person. It makes very good sense to me, and I know that it would work using the rise and the fall of a river. Why? Because of the push and pull of the water as it rises and falls. Also, I have had a few elders that have taught me this work.

Not only does my common sense tell me that this would work, but I also know for a fact that it works. It would be a long-term work until I removed it or until the string that was holding the jar or packet broke and the water removed it from the person.

This idea of bringing something to you by using running water also came out of the Hyatt books—to me it is just impossible. Some believe that because it came out of those books it is the truth and it will work. I personally would *never* use running water to try to bring something to me unless I collected the water in a jar when the water was rising, then the water could be tricked to draw whatever you were trying to draw in. I just don't see how it would work otherwise without also removing it from me at the same point—as in when the river goes down.

Think before you just jump in with both feet, and please always use your common sense. If this work would have been done for money or success, when the tide went out so would your money and success.

LAYING DOWN & DISPOSING OF TRICKS

In Conjure the herbs, roots, and other ingredients that are used to do a job should be disposed of once the job is done. This means anything that you have left over from your work. Where and how you dispose of the items really depends on the job and how it will be deployed. I was taught that if you want to give something *more* power, then throw or bury it in the east. If you want to destroy something or *weaken* it, you then bury or throw it to the west. The reason behind this is that the sun rises in the east and descends in the west.

Once you have laid your trick or disposed of the remnants, you should just walk away and forget about it. To look back on the work or to keep worrying about the work is the same as questioning its success; this can either weaken your work or kill it altogether—unless you are laying down powders as a trick. When you lay powders down, you walk backward sprinkling the powders in a zigzag motion. While you are sprinkling the powders, you pray your petition, being very forceful and making sure you call the target's name as you are laying them down. Once the powders are down, then you just walk away and forget about it.

There are many ways to lay a trick, but I want to share with you the way I do the work, even if I am only speaking for how I do it myself. One of my fondest memories of my mama is when my little brother caught her burying my dad's underwear behind the house right where my dad's feet would be if he were in bed. My mama was very tricky. My brother has never forgotten it—and I don't think he ever will.

I am very lucky; my home faces east and the back of my house is in the west. My home also sits on the corner of a crossroads, so I am doubly blessed. Understand that to bring something to you, you would work in the east, or maybe I should say any type of work you want to *grow* should be done in the east. Anything that you want to *decrease* or destroy should be done in the west. With that in mind, if you wanted to sour someone's luck and bring them down, you could take a whole lemon and cut it in half. Once this is done, place a name paper or photo of the target along with some red pepper and a pinch of sulfur in the lemon. Then add a little Confusion oil. Pin the lemon together with four pins. When you have the lemon pinned back together, take it and bury it in the west, where the sun sets. Make sure you mark the spot where you buried the lemon. Then go there daily as the sun is setting and pour a bit of vinegar on the spot. Remember to pray your petition while you pour the vinegar. This action will not only sour them, but it will bring them down just like the sun goes down in the afternoon.

Using this same idea, if you want to separate two people for whatever reason, get two lemons, name one for one target and the other one for the other target. Do the steps explained above, but this time you will place one lemon in the east and one in the west. You will then only feed the one in the west—the one you want removed. With this work, on your name paper, you will write one name going one way, and then turn your paper counterclockwise and write the other name going the other way. By doing this you are sending them in separate directions.

If you need to do a protection work, you can put together what I call a conjure jar or what some call a witch bottle, and then you can bury the jar by your front stoop. To make this type of jar, write out your petition. Then you need to add sharp objects to the jar: broken glass, nails, pins, a small pair of scissors, and so on. You can find tiny scissors in the miniature craft department of major craft stores. Scissors cut magic, so open the scissors when you place them in the jar. Once you have everything ready, you can add some holy water and bluing for protection. I have been asked in the past about adding your blood or personal concerns to this type of conjure bottle. *Do not add your blood!* This jar is made to repel your enemies with all the sharp objects you are placing in the jar; you *do not* want your life's force mingled with them. Once you have your jar made, you bury it near the front entrance to your home. Then once a month feed it a little fiery wall of protection wash to keep it working. (We've talked more about jars elsewhere in this book.)

Next let's talk about discharging a conjure work into running water. In my experience and from what I have been taught, the only time you would discharge a work into running water would be to *remove* something or someone from you. Why? Because water doesn't flow both ways—it doesn't move back and forth; it rises and falls. You can use your common sense to see how things line up. Here are a few examples. If I were doing a work to bring someone back to me, I would not throw the work into running water, because the water would *remove* them from me, not bring them *to* me. If I were doing a money conjure, I would not throw it into running water—not unless I wanted to jinx my money. By doing this I would be *removing* my money.

So when do we work with running water? When we want something to *go away*. If you are doing a separation work, law stay away, hotfoot, or protection of someone from another person, then you can throw the work into running water because you want to move these things away. As a worker it is very important that you understand this type of work; if you don't, you can be headed for trouble. *Always use your common sense.*

There is also one more work I would like to share with you along these lines of laying something down in water. If you have an enemy that just will not leave you alone, this is a good work for them. Everyone knows the river has an ebb and flow to it—meaning it rises and falls. Creeks are good for this work because they usually have stumps everywhere. I am gonna say this here to remind you—as I'll say many times throughout this book—you and you alone are responsible for the works you do. Make sure this work here is justified. This is a good work to teach someone a lesson, but only with good reason.

Make a packet up with the target's photo and any personal concerns you may have of theirs. Work the packet for nine days by praying your petition over it. On the tenth day take the packet to the creek, and use twine to tie the packet to a stump or tree limb that is in the water. The ole folks call this "fishing." I've heard my elders say before, "I'm gonna take so and so fishing" when I've never seen them hanging out and know they don't like each other. The reason for this work is that as the water goes out, the target gets a break from the work but, when the tide comes in and is high, they get hit with the work.

Some folks will leave the work there for a while and then set the target free, but I have an elder who would just leave it there as a punishment until the water rotted the packet and the twine—and only at that time would the work be undone. This is not the type of work you do because someone made you mad or because you simply don't like someone—this is more serious.

The only time I would bury a job in the graveyard would be to hold an enemy down or if I meant to harm someone. But I am going to be very honest here and say I have *never* placed work in the graveyard when I meant for another person to be harmed. There are other ways of dealing with someone than trying to maim or kill them. As to burying work in the graveyard and asking a spirit to hold the work there until I come back for it—yes, I have done that many times. If I can't make it to the graveyard, I will place the person in a box along with graveyard dirt and some other things and ask a spirit to hold them in the box. I only do this type of work in extreme situations. This is not something to be played around with. You need to be very careful and really think about what you are doing before you do this type of work.

Some workers will use food or drink as a way to deploy a trick. I personally have never done this, but my mama did. When I was in my early twenties, my sisters and I were sitting in the kitchen while mama was at the stove cooking. I happened to look up on the icebox and saw a bottle that said saltpeter on the label. I had never seen it before and wanted to know what it was, so I asked my mama. My oldest sister looked up to see what I was talking about and busted out laughing, while mama explained to me that the saltpeter was a *vitamin*—of all things—that my dad had to take. I couldn't understand why my sister was laughing so hard until she leaned over and told me what saltpeter would do.

I can tell you I was shocked to say the least. I didn't get a good explanation from my sister at that time because my mama gave us one of her looks that meant drop it or else. It wasn't until my mama passed in the 1980s that I really understood about saltpeter. We were all sitting around talking about mama and how she knew everything that was going on, and my sister brought up the saltpeter. Of course, we all had a good laugh about it, but I also got my explanation on why someone would work with it. Trust me when I tell you it is *not* a vitamin. Saltpeter is fed to a man to control or tie a man's nature. Once my sister explained the how and why it was used, I knew my mama was feeding it to my dad—but trust me, she had good reasons.

This will be our last example of laying a trick: the dressing of hats, clothes, and bedding. About twenty years ago I had a problem that I thought was getting out of control. Family is all good and fine, but sometimes their influence can be damaging to a marriage. Sometimes they stick their noses where they don't belong. I'm not one to let things go on for too long without doing something about it. So I decided I was going to get some control back again. I went to a shop in Houston to get some things I needed, and the lady asked me what the problem was. I explained what was going on. She suggested that I try an oil she had there in her store. Its name was Sister Edna's hat oil. I still have a half of bottle. To use the oil you place a few drops on the hatband, then pray your petition to gain control of whatever situation is going on. It worked and worked fast.

You can also dress clothing the same way. I like to dress the collars of their shirts or their socks. You can also dress their shoes. I like to use powders for this and just a drop of oil. The powders are easy—just sprinkle them on and brush off the excess. If I am doing a pair of shoes, I lift up the insole and place the powder and oil under the insole of the shoe. Another trick using the insole of a shoe is to write the person's name on a piece of paper that has been dressed with oil and powders and place it in the insole of the shoe. By doing this you are keeping them underneath your foot.

You can also dress your bed. This can be done by using oils or powders or placing a conjure hand under the mattress. The types of oil and powders you use would depend on the type of work. To dress your bed, dress the four corners with oil and the center of the bed with powder, sprinkling the powder in the pillowcase of the one the work is intended for. If you're going to place a conjure hand (which we will get to next), then put it under the mattress at the head of the bed.

CONJURE HANDS

Conjure hands are nothing more than a work you carry on your person. These hands are carried on you out of sight from prying eyes. They are hidden in your clothes up against your body. I pin mine at my waist inside of my underwear. Not all folks believe they need to be touching your body, but this is the way I was taught to carry them. It is up to the worker what instructions they give or follow. Some say these hands should not be seen or touched by others—if they are, then the hand will no longer work. This is what some workers call "killing a hand," and if it happens, a new one will need to be made.

Some folks call these hand mojo bags. I have always called them hands because they give you a helping hand in the situation they are made for. There are a variety of hands that can be made. I'm going to list a few here in this book, but this is by no means all of them. You can make a hand for protection, money, love, domination, controlling, mastery—you get the idea. It all depends on the type of work you need. Of course, one type for the topic of this book would go along the lines of mastery, controlling, compelling, and so on.

To make a love hand, you need a square of red flannel, about a four-by-four inch square, and some cotton string to tie the hand up. You need your petition that you've burned to ash, calamus root, lovage root, and rosemary. Place all the ingredients on top of the flannel. You then say your personal prayer and petition over the ingredients and gather the four corners together and wrap the string tight around the bundle. If you need to be in control, then you add calamus, licorice root, and Master of the Woods.

Once you have your hand made, it has to be fed. There are a few ways to do this. I am going to tell you how I do it, then give you a few more examples on how else it can be done. The most important thing is that *it is done* so the hand will be woken up to work.

When the hand is ready, before it is closed up, give the ingredients a few drops of whiskey, then breathe three breaths inside the hand. Close it up, then dab a little conjure oil on the outside of the bag. It just takes a little; you do not have to soak the hand. Once this is done, hold the bag close to your mouth and pray your prayer and petition into the bag while you squeeze the bag gently. My grandma called this whispering, and this is the way I was taught to wake up a hand.

Some workers smoke the hand with a cigar, incense, or the flame of a candle. Once you have smoked your hand, you need to give it a drink. Here are some things you can use: whiskey, oil, Hoyt's cologne, or bodily fluids depending on what the hand is made for. Some workers will even use sexual fluids if the bag is for love or the domination of a lover. Just a dab or two will do; you don't have to soak the hand. Once the hand is awakened, you carry it on you at all times. I even sleep with mine pinned to my nightclothes. You have to remember to keep the hand fed and to pray your prayers and petition into it at least once a week. Below are a few hands to give you an idea of what they contain.

Domination/Controlling Hand

Master root

Calamus root

Licorice root

Dirt dauber nest

Personal concerns

Petition paper

Master Hand

Master root

High John root

Solomon's seal root

Master of the Woods

Personal concerns

Petition paper

OFFERINGS

Let's be honest with ourselves for a minute: no one works for nothing. You wouldn't do a job that you never got paid for. So why in the world would we expect Spirit to do what we ask without pay? I know that Spirit will work for you even if you don't leave an offering, but it will work much better for you if you do. Not only by leaving an offering are you paying Spirit, but you are also showing honor, respect, and love. Spirit loves us enough to come when we call for help. Shouldn't we in turn love Spirit enough to honor it with a gift?

When you go to your job, you work hard because at the end of the week you know you will get your paycheck. Then why would we think Spirit doesn't want to be paid at the end of a job? I always promise my spirits an offering when the job is done. Like us, they want their pay; therefore they work harder to reach the goal. Sometimes I will give them the offerings in advance. I don't hold offerings back from my spirits trying to make them do something for me. I never try to control them. I honor them and respect them. So when you next do a job, tell Spirit when the job is done with good results, you will make an offering or just give the offering up front. It has been my experience that you will see a big difference. You can offer anything you want to. Spirit will accept it graciously because you gave the gift with love and appreciation. You can't go wrong.

The trick is to do a divination on the job first—that way you know if it will be a success or not. Don't just go to Spirit when you need something. Take the time to visit with your spirits when you don't need anything. When it is time to pay Spirit, tap three times on your altar, calling the spirits' name on each tap. Hold the offering up high; tell Spirit you have kept your word. You give the offering with love, honor, appreciation, and respect. Thank them for their help. Talk to them a little while and build a bond with them.

The more you go to your spirits, the easier it will become to reach them. Eventually all you will have to do is call on them and they will come. Leave the offering on your altar for a while, then dispose of it. Do *not* leave spoiled food and drinks on the altar; remove them before they go bad. Also keep a clean glass of water on your altar for them at all times. This draws spirits in but also refreshes them. Once a week light a small white stick candle in their honor to show that you care about them even when they are not helping you. If you do these small things, you will have success in all your work. They will be happy to come to you.

Anything you feel drawn to offer can be offered. Flowers, whiskey, cigars, stones, money, prayers—whatever you can offer will work. If I pay with whiskey, I leave it there until it is gone. I leave any stones or money I may have offered on the altar; they belong to Spirit unless I feel called to do something else with them. Try this next time you need assistance; I think you will see a big difference in the outcome of your work. No matter how much of your own energy you use in your work, you will never be as powerful as the spirits. So why not work and bond with them. It will make everything work with greater speed, and success is assured.

ENEMY WORK

There are times in our lives when we have to remove someone from our environment for whatever reason. Sometimes they just do not want to go, or maybe they are causing us problems and they have to be removed. This type of work should not be done on a whim or taken lightly. This is serious work; it should only be done if it is justified—in other words you need to have a good reason. I only use this type of work when all else fails—unless there is a threat to me or my family. If this is the case, I can promise you there will be no hesitation on my part to deploy this type of work. As a rule for me, though, in a normal situation I will try other things first. You have to remember that if this work is not justified and the target does a reversal or a call for justice, your ass will get slammed with your own work.

Here are a few things you can try to keep someone from coming around you before you use harsher measures such as hotfoot. You can place a broom behind your door with the broom handle down and the straw head pointing upward. You can say a petition to keep unwanted visitors from your home while standing the broom up behind the door. You can wait until they leave your home and make a circle going counterclockwise around the chair they sat in with a mixture of red pepper and salt. You do this while praying your petition that they do not return. Then you sweep this mixture out the door they left through all the way to the road. You can also sprinkle a mixture of salt and red pepper behind them as they leave while praying your petition that they do not return. Then take your broom and sweep it all the way to the road.

If all else fails, then move on to hotfoot, running water, or some other type of work to get them away from you. When someone is truly an enemy, the following works are things to do to justifiably deal with it.

To Nail an Enemy Down

There are times when folks just do not know when to stop and for whatever reason we need to stop them. One of the easiest ways to do this is to nail them down. What this means is they cannot do anything. They cannot move forward unless you make your petition where you just want them to leave you alone. There are a few ways I have done this.

A Simple Work to Nail Them Down

First, I am going to give you a simple way. You need a hammer, a railroad spike, and a picture of the person or a written petition with the person's name put down nine times going away from you.

Take your hammer and other items to the west side of your yard. Facing the west, place the picture or petition paper face down on the ground. Put the spike over the picture or petition, and, with the hammer, strike the spike three times, driving it into the ground. On each strike call the person's name and tell them they are nailed down and whatever else you want to happen. Mark the spot, and once a month take your hammer and hit the spot where the spike is while praying your petition. By doing this you are reinforcing your work.

You will be praying your petition for them to never come back, and you are nailing them down so they cannot possibly return. If you ever decide that you forgive them and want them to come back into your life, then just go and dig up the work. You would then do a cleansing and blessing on the spike to set them free of the work. I hardly ever undo any work I have done like this. If you have pushed me this far for me to nail you down, I doubt much has changed, so I'm gonna leave the work right where it is.

If you do not have a yard, you can work with a flowerpot. I have one on my breezeway that has been there for a while now. You can hammer your spike down into the soil and then you plant a plant in the pot that has hardy roots. As the roots of the plant grow, they will tangle up around the spike. The only way for the spike to get free would be for you to cut the roots of the plant. So therefore, the person the spike is named for cannot get free of the work. The larger the plant grows, the stronger the roots will become and the stronger the work will be. Some works take time, and you have to have patience. If you work with the pot, it may seem like it is not working, but as the plant grows, so will the work.

A Second Spiking Work

You need a railroad spike and a black marker. Write the target's name that you want to nail down on the railroad spike nine times. Stay focused on what you want to happen, pray your prayer and petition the whole time you are writing the target's name on the spike. When it is time for the sun to set, take the spike and go outside. Face the west and hit the spike in the ground one time saying,

> Just as the sun sets in the west so will you be set down.

Hit the spike a final blow driving it into the ground saying,

> The same way the sun can't rise in the west neither can you!

If you ever want to let them up, then pull the spike up. Clean the spike with holy water. Bless the spike in the name of God the Father, God the Son, and God the Holy Spirit. Then take it to the east side of the yard and on the first hit say,

> As the sun rises in the east so shall you.

On the final hit say,

> As the sun shines in the east so shall you shine.

To Be Rid of an Unwanted Person

Write the person's name on a piece of paper nine times. Then write on top of their name what you want to happen. Next burn the paper and mix the ashes with the hotfoot recipe. Make sure you wear gloves for this type of work. You do not want to hotfoot yourself or a loved one. Then go to every crossroad between your home and the home of the person you wish to be rid of, and while calling their name three times at each crossroad, pray your prayers and petition while sprinkling a little of your mixture. Take a different route home and forget about it. *It is done!* You need to do a good cleansing bath after this work.

Hotfoot Recipe

Red pepper

Cornstarch

Ant mound dirt and ants

A glass jar with a lid

Gather the ants and the ant mound dirt. Place them in the jar. Close the lid tight and leave the jar closed for about twelve hours.

Once the ants are not trying to get out of the jar anymore, add the red pepper. Shake the jar until it is mixed well. Now add your cornstarch. Shake the jar well. Now you should have a nice pink powder. Keep the lid on the jar tight to keep the dampness out.

More Hotfoot

I've just given you the recipe for my hotfoot powder. Earlier in the book I also gave you a couple of examples on how to use the powder in jar conjure and incorporating crossroads. I will only hotfoot someone if everything else I have tried has failed. You have to be very careful using this recipe; it is strong, and it truly works. You should never do a work if you do not know what you are doing. It has taken me over forty years to get the skills I have, and I am still learning.

If you don't know what you are doing, don't use it, particularly as a sprinkle!

You could end up putting the hotfoot on yourself, someone in your household, or the person you are trying to help. I have two clients who did this to themselves by sprinkling the powders and getting it on themselves. They both literally hotfooted themselves right out of their homes. One left hers for over a year, and the other one sold her house and land that was paid for.

Not every case is the same or is worked the same. It all depends on what the divinations say and where Spirit leads. One of the ways this powder can be used is as a sprinkle. I must caution you this can backfire if it is not done right. This type of work is not for the novice, nor is it to be taken lightly. You would sprinkle the powder where you are sure the target will walk. You should wear gloves to deploy this trick. While you are sprinkling the powder, you call their name three times, pray your prayer and petition, and tell them to leave. I would advise that if you use my recipe, you use it in a jar, then you throw the jar in running water. If you decide to lay this type of trick, make sure you clean your shoes with ammonia to kill the trick. Use extreme caution with this type of trick.

Hotfoot Jar

If I decide I need to make a hotfoot jar, I will write the person's name nine times going away from me on a piece of brown paper that I have drawn a circle on. Since the circle has no beginning and no ending, it is like a barrier. There is no way to get in or out of it. I place enough of the powder to cover the bottom of the jar. Then I put the name paper on top of the powder. Then I add another layer of hotfoot powder on top of the name paper. Then I will fill the jar the rest of the way with vinegar.

Once the jar is sealed, I will work the jar for a few minutes. To do this you call the person's spirit while shaking the jar, and you demand that they leave. I then give the jar to the client and advise them to work the jar for three days. Then take the jar and five pennies to running water and throw them in while giving thanks to the water spirit for removing the person from their lives.

Hotfoot Candle

The hotfoot candle I make was a gift from Spirit. I had a client come to me who was in a bad situation. She had someone in her home that she could not get rid of. I worked on this person for a little over six months. Everything I knew to make him leave only worked for a short while. He would leave, but within two weeks' time he would be right back in the home. I can tell you as a worker not everything works every time. But as determined as he was to stay, I was just as determined he was going to leave. So the battle continued until I was ready to call it quits. I finally told my client that I was at the end of my rope and she would have to find someone else to help her because nothing I did seemed to have worked. I made coffee, and we sat at my kitchen table talking. She is an old client I have worked off and on for over the years.

She just wouldn't give up, so I finally told her to let me pray on it and see what the spirits had to say about it. I make and sell candles. Some are working candles, and some just smell really good. I had a large order I needed to pour, but by the time she left, I needed a nap. I fell asleep with the candles I had to make on my mind. I dreamed of making a deep dark red candle I had added hotfoot powder to. I woke myself up talking to this candle and calling on the warrior Black Hawk. It was so real it didn't seem like a dream at all.

I got up and made myself a fresh cup of coffee, sat down at my kitchen table, and told Spirit to basically lead the way and

I would follow. I wrote his name inside a circle nine times, and then I burnt the name paper. I mixed the ashes with a small amount of the hotfoot powder minus the sulfur. I melted the wax, then I added the darkest color red I had to it. I put the hotfoot in the jar and called on Black Hawk to give the candle the power to drive away and defeat this enemy. Then I poured wax over the ingredients as I continued to talk to Black Hawk.

Once the wax had hardened, off and on the rest of the day I would pick up the candle and talk to it. The next morning, I went to my Black Hawk bucket and called him. (In case you don't know, Black Hawk sits in a bucket or foot tub, and that is where all his tools and statue are kept. Any work that is done with him is done within that space.) I lit the candle and left it burning. This time the job stuck, and I was given a gift by Spirit.

Is it right or just to use hotfoot on someone? Some will say that it is wrong; I say it depends on the situation. You will have to decide what is right for you and what is wrong for you to do. If you decide to hotfoot someone, just be very careful that you don't end up hotfooting yourself. Just remember all unjustified works will be reversed and your behind will get hit if you decide to do anything unjust.

To Block, Bind, and Return

If someone is really causing trouble and nothing you do seems to work, then this work should help you. There are some people you just cannot be good to. They live on making other people miserable. You know the ole saying "misery loves company." They seem to be able to stir up as much crap as they can, and they are never to blame. They basically get off scot-free of their actions. People do not see them as they really are. Folks never believe they are so underhanded and shady because they cover it so well. We are around folks like this all the time in our daily lives.

Well, this little mirror trick will not only bind them but will also turn all their ugliness back on them. They will have to look at their ugliness in the mirror every day—because no matter which way they turn, all they will see is themselves and their ugly ways.

You need a photo of the person, two small mirrors, and some black thread. Say your prayer and petition over the photo, then place the photo between the two mirrors with the backs of the mirrors facing outward.

Bind the mirrors with the black thread. As you wrap the mirror, stay focused and continue to pray your prayer and petition on each turn of the thread. They will be trapped inside of the mirrors, and everything they do will be reflected back on them. All they will see is themselves and their ugliness. They will be trapped in a world of their own making. Folks will begin to see exactly who and what they are. This may seem very simple, but it is a powerful work. No matter which way they turn, they will see only themselves.

When they have learned their lesson, you can release the work by cutting the thread and taking the photo from between the two mirrors.

To Cause Confusion

There are times when we just want someone to leave us alone. We don't want to harm them; we just want them to forget about us. I have found that the easiest way to do this is very simple. If you have a picture of the person, then you can use it for the job, but if you don't have a picture of them, that's okay. If you don't have a picture, then you need to get a large piece of brown paper bag and your scissors.

Draw a little dollie on the brown paper bag, and then cut it out. Draw a face on your dollie using a black permanent magic marker. When you have your dollie drawn, then you need to name it after the target. The next step is to dress the head of the dollie with Confusion oil. Look the dollie in the face and state your petition. Tell the dollie that they will forget about you—you will not even cross their mind. Then turn the dollie upside down and tack it facing a wall. This not only confuses the person the dollie represents, but it also blocks them from harming you. Any time you place someone up against the wall they cannot move against you; they are blocked by the wall.

If you are lucky enough to have a picture of the person, then draw a circle around the head in the photo and dress their head with the Confusion oil. Then place them upside down against the wall. This may seem like a simple trick—that's because it is—but it works. If you were able to come into my workroom, you will find a few of these. Once the person leaves you alone, you can remove the picture or dollie if you want to. Burn the paper to ash and take it outside and blow it to the east with a blessing on the winds for the target.

Not every work has to have a million candles or a huge list of supplies. Remember this work comes from a time when folks worked with what they had. Some of the simplest works are the most powerful ones. Don't get all caught up in all the hoopla—keep it simple.

War Water

In the old days, War Water was thrown against an enemy's door. If you try that today, you might go to jail. As times change, we must adapt the work. *War Water* means exactly what it says. It is used in a campaign to start a war against another person. In days gone by, the War Water was prepared in mason jars, and the whole thing was busted up against the enemy's door or on their stoop. In this day and time that would definitely not be a very good idea—there are cameras over practically every door stoop. But you can use the same technique, just in a different way.

The ingredients in the water are what make the water work. I understand the reasoning of busting the jar against the door: glass cuts, not only that but there is a violent element of throwing the jar at the door. You can get the same effect without busting the jar. Instead, use War Water as a sprinkle, by laying a trick on the person with whom you have a conflict with.

I had a problem some years ago with an in-law who was causing major problems for my sister. The whole family was in an uproar because this messy little woman could not stop stirring up trouble. She was very jealous of my sister and at every turn kept things stirred up. I tried to talk to her. I even did some light work on her.

The work would last for a while, then we were right back where we started. I knew about War Water, but there was no way I was going to throw a mason jar at her door. For one thing, I could not have done it and gotten away without getting caught. One night I was sitting outside during a real bad thunderstorm. Lightning was flashing and the thunder was so bad it shook the ground. I thought, well, thunder shakes and lightning burns, so why not make the War Water out of the rainwater from the storm.

I went inside, got me a bucket, and caught me some water. The next day I added some rusted nails my husband had in his shop, some broken glass, rose thorns (because they prick and make you bleed), needles, and dirt where three dogs had fought in a yard. While the water was setting, I went every day three times a day and worked the jar, making my petition for the purpose of the water.

I let the water sit until it became stagnant, then I put a little in a Coke bottle and went for a visit. The minute I stepped out of my truck I started sprinkling the water. I emptied the rest on the porch while praying my petition. I went inside, sat down, had a cup of coffee, then left. Needless to say, she is not in the family anymore and doesn't have any contact with my sister at all.

You can adapt anything to make it work without changing the meaning of the work. Do not get yourself in trouble trying to follow an old way of doing things when you can just do the work a little differently and have the same effect.

Swallowing an Enemy

This job is a double-edged one: the belly gets full and the enemy gets flushed. We all know that what goes in our mouth must come out the other end. So this work is done to ruin an enemy and move them away from you. Today we have toilets which take our waste away from us. In the old days they had outhouses where the waste just set there—which means the target just sat in a pile of waste while their life went to crap.

This job is kind of twofold because not only do you eat a beef tongue, you also have to skin it before you fry it up. I make this for my husband minus the work, so I am gonna give you my recipe for cooking tongue. You can try the recipe without the work, and it is pretty good. You can also leave out the red pepper if you don't like spicy food.

Consider your petition to Spirit about ruining your enemy and moving them away from you. Then let's get cooking.

The first thing you need to do is wash the tongue in some cool running water.

If this is for work, you name the tongue after the target and you pray Proverbs 18 V 20-21 over the tongue three times.

PROVERBS 18 V 20-21
20 From the fruit of their mouth a person's stom-
ach is filled; with the harvest of their lips they
are satisfied.
21 The tongue has the power of life and death,
and those who love it will eat its fruit.

Season a pot of water extra heavy. I add salt, red pepper, garlic powder, onion powder, and a diced onion. Pray the Proverbs 18 V 20-21 over the water, then add the tongue. I let the pot come to a hard boil and go for a while, then I lower the heat. Let the tongue cook for three to four hours, then turn the heat off and let the tongue cool. Be careful not to burn yourself. Once the tongue is cooled off, you need to strip the top layer off the tongue. As you are skinning it, you name the target and say your prayer and petition; you also pray the Proverbs 18 V 20-21 over it. Once you have the tongue clean, you can slice it into bite-size pieces. Some folks will soak it in a little buttermilk and egg mix. Then you lightly flour it.

Add a little oil to a skillet and let it heat. Then you add the tongue and cook it until it is golden brown. I remove mine from the skillet and sauté an onion with a little flour to make a gravy. Season to taste. Then I place the tongue back into the skillet and let it simmer on a low heat until it is tender. You should be praying your petition and speaking the target's name as you are cooking. Make a pot of rice, and when the tongue is done, you will have a nice meal of rice and gravy with tongue. Enjoy your meal and forget about them once you are finished. What you want is a done deal.

GRAVEYARD WORK

Graveyard dirt can be used in many ways. It can be used in protection, love, crossing, and domination work just to name a few. I have heard about many ways to use graveyard dirt over the years. Some say there are certain times to go to the graveyard, certain phases of the moon, what days one should collect on, the list goes on and on. I go any time I need to petition the spirits for help. I am not going to wait until the full moon or whatever if I have a job that needs to be done. The only rule I do follow—and this is my own rule—is that I won't petition help from spirits who are not my kin or I didn't know in life.

Why? I am not going to ask some unknown spirit to help me. To do so is very foolish and very dangerous. You should only petition spirits you have a bond with. Use your common sense. Just because a person has passed on does not mean that they have all of a sudden become a good person. Their spirit is the same, maybe even stronger, now that they have passed. I'm going to give you a little example of what I am talking about.

My brother got into a little trouble with the law. I live about an hour's drive from the graveyard where my parents are buried. My brother was off working at the time, so he couldn't go get the dirt for me. I couldn't leave to go get it either, so I asked his girlfriend if she would go get it and bring it to me. She agreed to go for me even though she had never done anything like this before.

I explained to her everything she needed to do. I talked to my parents at my altar and explained everything to them. I told them why I couldn't go to them myself. I felt like every-thing would go well—wrong. I called her and told her to go ahead and go get the dirt. I told her to talk to them to tell them again why she was there. Well, when she got back home, she called me and told me about her experience.

She did everything like I told her to. She got the dirt off my mama's grave just fine, but when she went to get dirt off my daddy's grave, she had a real hard time just getting a few scoops. Now these graves are side by side. She should not have had a problem. The problem was my dad did not want her get-ting the dirt even though she was getting it for my brother so I could help him. Why? My dad didn't approve of her when he was alive, and it hadn't changed even though he had passed on. He was set in his ways when he was living. Now that he has gone on, his spirit hasn't changed.

He let her get just enough dirt for me to do what I had to do in order to help my brother. Why am I telling you this little story? I want you to understand that just because some-one has passed on it does not mean that they are any dif-ferent than they were when they lived. If they were mean, hardhearted, cold, thoughtless, or heartless when they lived, they are still like that in spirit—maybe even more so. It is not my intention to frighten you. I just want you to use common sense when dealing with the spirits of the dead. They can and will help you in your work; just be sensible in which spirits you ask.

Approaching the Graveyard

I want to explain how I approach the graveyard when I need to collect dirt or do work. Every worker has his or her own way of doing this. One way is not better than the others. This is my way; you have to decide the right way for you. There are only two things that I stand firm on and I think everyone should do before and after you go to collect dirt or do work in the graveyard. Number one is before you go to the graveyard you need to take a good protection bath and even have a good protection amulet on your person. Number two is that when you return home you need to do a good cleansing.

Let me explain to you why I follow these two rules. Let's face the facts. Spirits roam the graveyard; that is where they live. Folks who don't know better assume that all the spirits are in the graves. This is absolutely not true—there are spirits in the graveyard that are not in graves. Some call them the spirits of the place, and others call them the dead—either way they are still there roaming around. Not all of them are happy about passing on. Some of them can be very nasty.

You need to also understand that when you go there you will be building energy with your prayers or whatever you plan to do. Entities are drawn to this energy you are putting out. Why in the world would you go there without protection? Please use your common sense. Now you've done your work, and you go home. Maybe nothing attached itself to you—or maybe it did. You might have picked something up or you might not have. Why would you take a chance? Cleanse yourself just to be on the safe side. It is better to be safe than sorry.

Once I have my protection bath, I gather whatever I need to bring with me. Then I go to my ancestor altar. I call on my spiritual protector and my ancestors. I ask them to keep me safe. I explain to them about the work I will be doing. I say my prayers, and then I leave to go to the graveyard. The whole time I am driving to the graveyard I am praying. Not only that I be protected, but also that the work I will do will be a success.

When I get to the road that leads to the graveyard, I leave an offering. I call to the keeper of the gate and ask permission to enter. By the time I reach the gate I know if I can go in or not. Then at the gate I will leave another offering. I usually leave three pennies. I can't stress enough how important it is to be respectful when you enter the graveyard. You are there to ask for assistance. *Ask* is the key word here.

When I reach the grave, the first thing I do is say a prayer for them. Then I will talk to them for a while. Even though I will be paying for the work or dirt, no one likes to feel used— not even the spirits. When I feel the time is right, I will tell them what I need help with. At this point it is important that you *listen*. Why? Well, there have been a few times when I was led to do something different than what I had planned on doing. Not only did the work turn out right, but also it was very powerful.

One of the jobs has lasted over ten years. I guess you could call me the keeper of my family. When things go wrong, I'm the one they come to. One of my brothers got into some trouble trying to help someone out. He was where he should not have been to start with, but I guess that is beside the point. Anyway he got jumped on by two brothers. You know the type; tough guys when a friend is around. Well, needless to say, they came out with the raw end of the deal. Their daddy had always been the type of man who does not see his children as being wrong ever. If you messed with his kids whether they are wrong or right, he'd come after you.

One night my younger brother calls me. He says, "Sister, I need to tell you something." I knew the minute I heard his voice something was wrong. He talked. I listened until he finished. I asked if my brother had called the police and told them what was going on. He said no, that he thought it would just blow over. What happened was the boys went home and lied to their daddy. They told him my brother jumped them. One against two! How smart would that have been?

Anyway as the story goes, the old man went looking for my brother with a gun. Thank God he didn't find him. I was past furious when I heard this. I called my brother to find out what really happened. Sure enough, word had gotten back to him that the old man was hunting him. We were raised to respect our elders, so when I asked my brother what he was going to do, he said, "I'm not going to do anything. I don't have a problem with that old man." I told him, well, I have a problem with him. Nobody threatens my family. He let me rant and rave until I ran out of steam.

He was going out on a job in a few days and would be gone for a while. He thought everything would have cooled down by the time he got back. I knew better. We had heard tales about this mean ole guy our whole lives, so I knew he wasn't going to just let it go. So when I hung up with my brother, I started thinking of what could be done not only to save my brother but also to stop the old man from ruining his own life over a lie.

I don't usually work when I'm upset because I'm not sure what I might do. This night was different though. I made a wax dollie and named it for the old man. I taped his eyes and his hands then used Confusion, Controlling, and Domination oils. I bound the dollie with black thread, and then I nailed him in a small black box. It was my intention to take him to the graveyard, bury him there, and never go get him out again. At that point I really didn't care what happened to him. I didn't dare work on his sons. I was too furious. It's no telling what I would have done to them.

Sleep didn't come easy to me that night, and the next morning I went straight to the graveyard. There will be times that you will do work that you will never forget. For me this is one of those works. You should never do this type of work when you are angry or upset, especially if you are going to do graveyard work. I let my emotions override my common sense and my knowledge. I am so thankful that my mama took over and stopped me from doing something I would have been sorry for later on. I don't remember everything that happened that day. I do remember getting out of my truck and running to my mama's grave holding the box. I remember just falling to my knees holding the box and just babbling. I can't tell you how long I stayed there like that. The next thing I remember I was warm all over and at peace.

It was as if my mama were holding me as she had done when something happened to hurt or upset me. I swear I could hear her talking to me. She would not allow me to bury the box. She said she would take care of things. She told me to go home and to do a work that would open the old man's eyes so he would see the truth and she would take care of the rest. I went home and called my brother and told him what happened. Then I went and did the work.

A couple of months went by and I would call him every now and again just to make sure everything was all right. Then out of the blue he called me one day. He said, "Sister, the problem is over. I don't know what you did or how you did it, but it worked." I said, "What are you talking about?" He had run into the old man the night before, and the old man asked if he could speak with him. My brother said he told him okay because he didn't have a problem with him and didn't want any trouble. The old man said he wasn't there to make trouble.

Come to find out more than one person had approached the old man and told him that his boys were at fault—that the both of them jumped my brother and he was just defending himself. He shook my brother's hand and told him that if his sons were ever stupid enough to do something like that again, then they deserved whatever they got, and he wasn't going to step into it. To this day, no matter where this man meets my brother, he speaks to him.

There are two very important lessons I learned here. One is to never let my emotions get control of my work, and number two is to always listen to what the spirits have to say. This could have turned out so very different—not only for the people involved but also for me. I was very lucky. So please think before you act. Every action causes a reaction, and when you are dealing with this type of work, you have to be careful. I could have really been harmed by going to the graveyard with my emotions so high. The fury I had boiling in me at that moment could have drawn a dark entity to me that could have attached itself to me. I shudder to think what could have happened. Just please think before you act.

Before we move on, I would like to say this: Don't just go visit the graveyard when you need help. Go on the holidays. Pick a grave to clean and add fresh flowers for the person resting there. Speak with the spirit of the person. Let them know they are not forgotten. One day you may need their help.

Collecting Graveyard Dirt

When I'm ready to get my dirt, I use my pendulum to find out where the best place is to get it. I always check myself. I have learned over the years this is a good habit to have. Sometimes I will get dirt from more than one place on the grave. It just depends on what the pendulum says. Once I did some work to drive someone away from my daughter. I had already made a wax dollie into which I had mixed hotfoot along with personal items and the ashes of my petition. This probably would have been enough, but I wanted to make sure the job was done fast.

I was going to take the dirt from the heart area of my mama's grave because she loved my daughter so much. I knew she would take care of the problem. Instead, I was led to take dirt from the left hand and foot of the grave. So once again the spirit changed the work to be done. The left hand explains itself, but it took me a while to figure out the foot thing. I was puzzled about that all the way home. Then like lights coming on, I remember my mama telling us many times that the best way to defeat someone is to walk on them—meaning put them under your foot. If someone is causing you trouble, you can write their name on a petition and either place it on the floor and stomp on it or wear it in your shoe to walk on them.

It doesn't take a lot of dirt to get the work done. I always just take a tablespoon or so. Once I get the dirt, I'll drop some coins in the hole where it came from. This pays for the dirt. I never give my mama whiskey; she was against any type of alcohol. So I always bring her strong black coffee. I will either place a cup in the hole and fill it with coffee or, if I forget to bring the cup, I will just pour the coffee in the hole. She smoked Pall Mall cigarettes, so I always bring her some. I will open the pack and light one. I give her three puffs, then place the cigarette on the edge of the hole so she can smoke some. I leave the rest of the pack for her. Once I give all the offerings, I will give thanks for the help given.

When I am at the gate, I also thank the gatekeeper for letting me in and for protecting me. I leave three more pennies on my way out. By leaving three more pennies at the gate. I know the gatekeeper will not let anything follow me. Once I drive out of the gate, I don't look in my mirrors until I am well away from the graveyard. I don't want to maybe draw a spirit to me that may be lingering outside the graveyard. Always be respectful of the spirits and always pay your debt to them. You really never know when you may need them.

We need to remember that graveyard work is a lot more than just enemy work. We also need to remember that when you go to the graveyard, it is important to protect yourself. I have found that some folks have been taught or believe that they can go to the graveyard and do their work without protection. This is a misconception. Before you go to the graveyard, you need to do a protection work for yourself. Common sense tells us this; you are entering the place where spirits live.

When you finish your work at the graveyard, you need to cleanse yourself. You don't want to take a chance that something might have followed you home. I always carry a spray bottle with me that has one cap of ammonia, kosher salt, and frankincense added to the water. I spray my feet and my body with this spray after leaving the graveyard while saying the Lord's Prayer. Once I get home, I do a good cleansing. It's always better to use caution when doing this type of work.

To Make a Person Leave

Here's a simple but effective way to make a person who is causing problems leave. Get you a white handkerchief, a red chili pepper pod—either fresh or dried, graveyard dirt, and your petition paper. The first thing you need to do is lay out your handkerchief, then you write the target's name nine times going away from you on your petition paper. Fold the paper away from you until it is a small cylinder. Set your petition aside for a minute. Cut the dried pepper pod longways. Then insert the petition into the pepper. Sprinkle the paper with graveyard dirt, and ask Spirit to remove this problem.

Place the pepper pod in the center of the handkerchief and fold the handkerchief in half folding it away from you. Then keep folding it until it is a small roll. Pick both ends of the bundle up and tie it in strong knots. On each knot state your petition. When this is done, take it to running water and throw it in while saying your prayers and petition. It is done! They will leave you alone after this.

ROOTS, HERBS & CURIOS

Roots, herbs, and curios are a huge part of this work. This list also includes dirts from different places, sticks, stones, water, and anything else you can think of. I'm not gonna put a list of herbs and such in this book—there is already plenty of information out there on them. I want to write about the things folks don't know about working with like different types of dirts, sticks, stones, and waters from different places. I decided I wanted to write things that most folks don't know about unless they have an elder who works the old way.

Back in the old days, powders were not what they are today. Powders were made out of talc, which today we know is very harmful, but back then it was the thing. My mama dusted our beds every night with either talc or cornstarch. Today most of the premade powders you buy are nothing more than powder that has been colored. Most folks nowadays don't add herbs and dirts to their powders. Back in the ole days the powders were mostly dirt with just a little talc added in. You have to understand the land wasn't always so covered with roads and cement; roads and yards were dirt except for in the city. If you would have tried to sprinkle the powders made today, they would have been seen, but the powders from that time went undetected because they were made more from dirt and didn't stand out when they were laid.

I still make these types of powders and I work with them. The only scent and color they have is from the herbs, ash from the Bible verse burned, and the dirt I use to make them. I'm gonna share a few recipes with you.

- Dirt from a place you find peaceful
- Powdered lavender
- Powdered calamus root
- 12 white candles
- James 3 V 18
- And a harvest of righteousness is sown in peace by those who make peace.

Mix the ingredients together in a bowl. Place four of the candles around the bowl starting at the top then the bottom then from left to right. Light the candles as you have laid them out. Pray the James 3 V 18 over the powder three times as this first set of candles burn. You will burn a set of candles for three days. On the third day burn the verse to ash and mix it with the other ingredients. Once the last set of candles burn out, the powder is ready. It only takes a little powder to do a trick.

This is an old powder, and I have never seen it written about. I'll share it here so the knowledge of it won't be lost. Remember what I said: we are all responsible for the works we do, and all works should be justified.

- Dirt from around the base of a weeping willow tree
- Cream of tartar
- Dirt from a disaster
- 12 black stick candles

- Psalm 42 V 3 My tears have been my food day and night, while they say to me all the day long.

Mix the ingredients together in a bowl. Place four of the candles around the bowl starting at the top then the bottom then from left to right. Light the candles as you have laid them out. Pray the Psalm 42 V 3 over the powder three times as this first set of candles burns. You will burn a set of candles for three days. On the third day burn the verse to ash and mix it with the other ingredients. Once the last set of candles burns out, the powder is ready.

You have to remember that the ancestors had no money and all they had to work with was what they had on hand. It was easy to trick a rock or a small tree limb and put it back where the target would come in contact with it. To the target it would look like a stick or a rock, but it would really be a trick laid. This type of trick can be worked for anything, you can move someone out by tricking a rock and leaving it on their door stoop or pulling some leaves off of a tree in the target's yards then taking them and tricking them. When the work is ready, you just go put them in the target's yard. Simple, easy, and very powerful—this is real conjuring at its best.

There are many ways to trick water and water is easy to lay the trick down. To be a good worker you have to think like an elder. Think of how they lived, what they had to work with in their time. The older works are very powerful, but you have to get out of your modern-day thought forms. You hear a lot about taking things to running water or throwing things in water. What about bringing the water to the target after it has been worked? I have not read about this anywhere. I guess no elders are sharing this type of works with the public. I'm gonna give you a few examples of how water can be worked. I'm sure I am gonna be ridiculed for sharing this work in this book, but if I don't share it, then it will be lost.

To Stop Success

Stagnant water is water that is not moving—it just sits there and rots. This is the type of water you would work with to stop a target's success or to get them off a job. You simply gather the water in a jar with a lid on it. Bring the water to your work area, write the target's name on each of five stick candles, and then set the candles in a cross setup with a stick candle burning on top of the jar. Pray Job 26 V 7: "He stretches out the north over the void and hangs the earth on nothing." I would do this setup for at least nine days. Once the candles have all been burned, then the water is ready. You can take the water and pour it in the target's yard, near their job where they will walk in it, or go visiting and pour it out all the way to the door!

To Raise Love

What about love? Nowadays folks either care about money or love; these are at the top of most folks' list, along with success. Water comes in handy for this type of trick because you can spill it anywhere and the target will think you just spilt some water. Water is one of the easiest tricks to drop, yet many would-be conjure workers know nothing about this type of work! Collect some water from the river when the tide is up. Remember what I said earlier about the ebb and the flow of the water. When the tide is high, it brings the water into the bank, this is when you want to collect your water. You can watch the news to see when the tide is high or low. I would do this setup for twenty-one days. You will need five red stick candles to burn a day. Write the target's name on each of the candles. If you have their photo, you can burn it into ash, dress the candles in sweet oil, and roll them in the ash. Pray the Song of Solomon 8 V 7: "Many waters cannot quench love, neither can floods drown it." Place the candles around the jar starting from the top to bottom left to right because you want to nail the target down. Place one of the candles on top of the jar. Once the candles have all been burned, then the water is ready.

These old works really do work! There is no hocus pocus, just prayers and candles. Deploy them with wisdom!

SHUT YOUR MOUTH CONJURE

Let's face the facts: folks love to gossip. Nowadays it seems like everyone is on the gossip train—it is even worse in the so-called spiritual community. Some folks seem to have nothing better to do with their time than to gossip and lie about other folks. They don't seem to care about the damage, hurt, and pain their lies can cause the person. I'm not even sure they care; it seems like almost everyone gossips. It is sad! The last thing anyone needs is other people prying into their business. How many loving relationships has this type of meanness hurt?

These types of people are everywhere. You find them on the job, in families, and on the internet. We all need to know how to stop those who would gossip and lie on us. They need to get a taste of their own medicine and have their actions turned back on them. We have to remember every action causes a reaction—not only that words hold power and they hurt. You can't take them back once they are spoken.

Tapa Boca/Shut Up Candle

Get a Shut Your Mouth candle, and using a permanent marker write the offender's name on the mouth that is painted on the candle. If you can't find one of these candles, you can draw a mouth using a black permanent marker on a glass-encased candle. Then get a piece of duct tape and put it over the name and mouth. While holding the candle in one hand, slap the mouth that is under the tape hard three times. On each slap tell the target they will shut their mouth. You have to be forceful. You can't just say, "Shut your mouth"—you have to put your willpower into the petition.

Then sprinkle a little calamus to dominate and a little alum to turn their mouth bitter every time they gossip about you on the candle and put the name paper down in the candle after you have made a little hole near the glass. Hold the candle up to your mouth, and call the target's name and say your petition. Then pray the prayer below over the candle, calling the target's name out after each stanza. Repeat the process three times. Place the candle in a metal can for fire safety and light it. Repeat the prayer and petition three more times over the lit candle. Tell them they will shut their mouth and keep it shut.

Try to say the prayer and petition at least three times a day while the candle is burning. You may have to repeat the burn if they continue to gossip about you.

Prayer to Stop Slander/Shut Up

> We need Thee, O Lord, to curb vicious tongues
> from making cruel judgments, vile criticisms,
> and untruthful statements.
> Dear Almighty God, silence our enemies. Keep
> them from speaking barbed words that cut
> into our hearts and souls. Make their unkind
> words fall upon deaf ears and shield us from
> their wickedness and evil.

O Lord, make us sweet inside that we may be
gentle with others, gentle in what we say, and
gentle in what we do. In Thine own strong
name we do pray. Amen.

Justice Against Gossip

I wanted to add a work for justice against the folks who gossip. This work is built on justice work and protection. Folks overstep themselves in this day and age; they don't respect themselves or anybody else. Any work that is justified can be done with no backlash from the work. That is why I only do justified work!

If you don't stand up for yourself, who else will do it? I know a lot of folks don't believe in this type of work. They believe that one should let karma tend to these types of folks. I personally feel like karma is too slow at times, and if the work is justified, it can and should be done! The only thing you have to remember is that you and you alone are responsible for any works you do. I have repeated this throughout this book because it is important that folks understand the responsibility of doing Conjure. These works may seem simple, but they are very powerful. Don't let their simplicity fool you.

I want to explain why the Proverbs 18 V 6-7 is worked with here. This work could be looked at as a crossing work *if* you were not justified in doing it because the target was gossiping about you. Since it is justified, you are simply asking for justice. The verse "the lips of fools bring them strife and their mouths invite a beating" is saying that by the target gossiping they are asking for strife and a spiritual beating to be brought down on their lives.

Next we have "the mouths of fools are their undoing, and their lips are a snare to their very lives." Here we see their mouths will be the end of them and they will be caught in their own traps. What better way to call justice down on a target who has caused so much pain with their gossip? Even if the gossip is true, folks are not allowed to harm others with words.

For me personally, I don't call names because I might miss someone who is hiding out. I say, "All those whose tongues gossip about me, be it true or nay; shut their mouths!" For this work I like to burn black stick candles; I like black because it absorbs—it pulls things off of you. I will burn on this for three, five, seven, or nine days. It all depends on where Spirit leads me. You will burn a candle a day and let it burn completely out. Here is what you need to do!

Don't dress the candle with any type of oil or powder. The goal of the candle is to pull off the hurt and pain you feel from the target and give it back to them. Brush yourself off with the black candle starting at the crown of your head down moving to the bottom of your feet. Try to do as much of your body as you can. Then hold the candle up to your mouth and pray Proverbs 18 V 6-7 into the candle.

> PROVERBS 18 V 6-7
> 6 The lips of fools bring them strife, and their
>   mouths invite a beating.
> 7 The mouths of fools are their undoing, and
>   their lips are a snare to their very lives.

Once that is done, place the candle in a fireproof bowl and light it.

Let the candle burn for a few minutes while you watch the flame. Then pray the prayer and your petition over the candle three times before it burns out. Do this work for at least three days, which means a candle a day for three days. You need to repeat the same process daily.

Protection Against Gossip

There are times when folks just will not leave a person alone. It does not matter how hard the person tries to mind their own business; it seems like folks are always talking about them or their family. This type of thing can not only be hurtful but damaging to their reputation. Everyone loves drama, don't they? Or do they? People are cruel sometimes, and it seems these folks just get off scot-free!

I wanted to share this simple work with you that can hide you from the gossip hounds and bring justice to those who can't seem to mind their business and keep their mouths shut! You will need a tin can for this work, two small mirrors to fit inside the tin can, and a photo of yourself, your family, or the front of your home. You need dirt from the four corners of the property and dirt from an ant bed.

Let me explain about the ant bed dirt. It may sound kind of odd, but remember ants travel—they move from place to place. You need for the gossiping loulous to move away from you and find a new nest to bother and leave your home alone. Ants also eat things up, and this is what needs to happen so the wagging tongues can feel the bite.

You will need to make a wash of bay leaf, four tablespoons of salt, and four tablespoons of baking soda so you can wash the mirrors and the can before you prepare them for the work. Mirrors are magical within themselves because they can capture not only your image but also a spirit or energy from someone who has handled them. Like the broom, mirrors are not to be played with. Once you have the wash made, bathe the two mirrors and the can with it and let them air-dry. The rest of the wash you can pour on your stoop.

Gather the dirt from the four corners of the property and the dirt from the ant bed, and place them in the dried can. Take the photo and place it in between the two mirrors with the mirrors facing outward. Make sure that you do not look in the mirrors. Place the mirror packet in the can on top of the dirt you collected. Hold the can up to your mouth and pray the Proverbs 11 V 9 into the can. Repeat the prayer and your petition three times into the can, then blow three breaths into the can. Set the can aside.

> PROVERBS 11 V 9
> With their mouths the godless destroy their
>   neighbors, but through knowledge the righ-
>   teous escape.

You need a red glass-encased candle. I like to work with a red candle for this because red is a hot color, but it also represents the blood and the power of the ancestors. If you don't want to burn a red candle, you can pick whatever color candle Spirit leads you to burn. Most folks load their candles full of oil and roots and herbs. I personally prefer to fill the wax with my prayers and my petitions because wax holds a memory and the fire of the flame heats up the power of the prayers and petition. If you would like to add some oils and ingredients to the candle, please feel free to do so.

Hold the candle up to your mouth, and say your petition three times into the wax. Then pray the Proverbs 11 V 9 into the wax three times and blow the three breaths into the wax.

Remember our breath holds our life force, which in turn holds the power to bring the candle to life. Light the candle and say your prayer and petition over the candle three times during the day. Then go daily and pray your prayers and petition over the candle until the candle burns out. I personally would do a twenty-one-day burn on the situation, but you could just let the one candle burn out and see how it goes.

Tongue on Fire

I think almost everyone has heard of the beef tongue work to stop gossip. Folks have run wild with that work. That really is the only work I have seen folks talk about or share photos of, but there are many works that are done using animal parts. You have to remember back in the days of slavery and up until the 1960s folks butchered their own meat. Some folks still do today although the practice is dying out because it is much easier to get processed meat at the grocery store.

Remember, enslaved ancestors did not get the best cuts of meat from the animals; they got what the slave master didn't want to eat. Nothing was wasted! Absolutely nothing! They learned to make the food taste good and some of the recipes are still cooked today in some families. They also worked with what they had—you didn't run to the store like folks do today back then. Even when I was growing up, my family went to town once a week on Saturday afternoons. I still go on Saturdays to buy what I need for the week since it is what I grew up doing.

This work is harsh—I am not even gonna try to sugarcoat it. But sometimes folks make you do harsh things. Liars are the scum of the earth, and they have destroyed the lives of many a folk. Families have been destroyed over lies and gossip. Folks have been murdered over lies and gossip; there are folks in prison who are innocent yet locked up because of lies, gossip, and hearsay! This work right here is not to be done lightly just because you are mad at someone or you think someone is talking about you. This is the kind of work you really need to be sure of before you set out to do it. I started not to add this work in this book, but then I thought, why not? We are all responsible for our actions. That is why I am trying to be very clear here and tell you not to mess around with this work if you are mad at someone.

This work should only be done in extreme circumstances. I am not trying to scare anyone; I am just being truthful. As you have probably guessed, this work effects the tongue of the liar and gossip—but it also affects their whole mouth. I have seen it affect the target's teeth, gums, and cause mouth ulcers and canker sores. So just be mindful. You cannot say I was not clear about the work or what might happen if you decide to do this work.

I want to say one more thing: just because you have the knowledge to do something does not mean you have to do it! Over the course of my learning years, I have been taught a lot of harmful works, but that does not mean I do them. I am a two-headed justified worker, meaning that I can bless as well as curse. I do not do anything that is not justified. Be responsible with your actions. Below is a list of items you need for this work.

A beef tongue

An aluminum pan

Dried red peppers

Powdered red pepper

A photo of the target

Cream of tartar

3 black stick candles

Castor oil

Black twine

Fire starter

Wash the beef tongue off in some cool running water to clear away what it might have picked up from folks handling it. Pat the tongue dry with some paper towel to remove all of the water. Cover the bottom of the aluminum pan with the dried red peppers, then place the tongue on the bed of peppers. Cut a slit in the top of the tongue and place the target's photo in the slit. Set the pan aside. Mix the powered red pepper and the cream of tartar together. The red pepper is to heat up the mouth, and the cream of tartar is to make the tongue bitter. Using a blade because you want to cut the tongue of the target, write the target's name on the three black stick candles. You can do them all at once.

You will name each of the candles for the target. *Do not* breathe on these candles—you do not want your life's force mixed with this mess. Rub some castor oil—which is for cursing—on the candles and then roll the candles in the powdered red pepper and the cream of tartar mix. You might want to bring the candles and the tongue outside in order to burn the candles because the red pepper becomes hot in the air when it is burned and you don't want to breathe that in. Hold both hands over the tongue and name the tongue after the target, repeating the naming three times. Then pray James 4 V 11 over the tongue three times calling the target's name three times after each sentence.

> JAMES 4 V 11
> Brothers and sisters, do not slander one another.
> Anyone who speaks against a brother or sister
> or judges them speaks against the law and
> judges it. When you judge the law, you are not
> keeping it, but sitting in judgment on it.

Stick one of the black stick candles into the slit you made in the tongue where you placed the photo. Light the candle and say your prayer and petition over the candle three times calling the target's name each time. Then pray the James 4 V 11 over it three times also calling the target's name. Try to repeat this three times before the candle burns out. You will repeat this until all three candles have burned out. You burn one candle a day for three days in a row. On the fourth day the work changes.

I want to explain about the number three. The number three represents the Holy Trinity and the ancestors. It is considered by some, myself included, to be a very lucky number. But there is also another reason it is important that most folks don't know about. It also represents the three nails that held Jesus on the cross—but that is not all. Did you know when Jesus died on the cross, his spirit went to hell? For how long? Yes, that is right: for three days! Most of my works are done in threes. Folks really understate the power of the works in the Bible because some Christians have turned it into a book of hate so folks are turned off by anything that has to do with Christianity! We should remember that churches are a man-made vessel and run by men, and the Bible is just a book! I just thought I would share that little gem with those who might not know.

After the three candles have burnt out, take the black twine and bind the tongue and the target. You can say something like this:

> I bind the tongue and *X* from speaking my name!
> May their mouth become bitter and burn
> every time they speak ill of me!

Just keep praying the petition over the tongue until the whole tongue is bound up tight. Then you repeat the James 4 V 11 and the petition over the tongue three more times. Once this is done, cover the tongue with fire starter and throw a match on it. Be very careful to stand away from the pan. Let it burn! Once the fire goes out and the pan is cool to the touch, you can either bury it, throw it in running water, or throw it in the woods for the animals to devour!

A Work for Busybodies

Below is a work I did for a client who was being gossiped about on the job. She almost lost her livelihood due to a couple of busybodies who could not stop running off at the mouth. I was not sure how I was going to handle the work. Sometimes when we think we know who is causing the problem, there are others hiding out of the way we don't even think would talk about us. Folks you wouldn't even consider would try to harm you could be spreading gossip and rumors about you.

I have made it a practice when I do this type of work not to call anyone's name. I always say, "All my enemies known and unknown." Spirit knows who has wronged you.

This way you do not harm someone who is innocent. I have a couple of variations I do of this work. It all depends on what Spirit leads me to do and what I see needs to be done.

To do this work, I made a dollie. The dollie was of very soft wax so the wax is easy to work with. While I was shaping the dollie, I thought about my client and the gossip and hurtful energies being directed at them. I never bless this type of work because the reason for doing the work is not to draw in blessing but to stop someone who is causing harm. Once I had the dollie shaped, I took a coffin nail and made holes for the eyes and the mouth. I made them kind of deep because I was going to stuff them. I saved the wax that I removed from the eyes and mouth because I was going to use it to plug up the mouth and close their eyes after the dollie was loaded. Once the dollie was made, I sprinkled it with water three times and said,

> I name you for all of *X*'s enemies known and
> unknown, whatever is done to you is done to
> them. Whatever affects you affects them.

Then I took the dollie back to my workspace. I filled the hole I made for the mouth with my red peppers, cream of tartar, and thorns, and then I stuffed the mouth with slippery elm. I then took a piece of the wax I had saved and sealed the mouth shut with it while praying Isaiah 54 V 17.

ISAIAH 54 V 17
No weapon forged against you will prevail, and
you will refute every tongue that accuses you.

And I also prayed my petition that my client's enemies' mouths be sealed. Then the next step was to fill the eyes with black mustard seeds, and I closed them up with a thin layer of wax too. I prayed the Isaiah 54 V 17 and my petition that they would not see my client. I prayed that they would be confused every time they saw my client. I also filled the head with black mustard seeds so they would stay confused when they thought of my client.

When all this was done and the dollie was ready, it was time for the next step. I made a wash with cream of tartar, calamus, black mustard seeds, and slippery elm. Once I had the wash done, I soaked two pieces of cotton material strips in the wash. One of the pieces I used to bind the dollie's hands so that my client's enemies couldn't work against them. I tied three knots while praying the Isaiah 54 V 17 and my petition that they could not lift a hand against my client. Then I wrapped the mouth and the head with the other one and prayed the Isaiah 54 V 17 and my petition that they would not see or speak of my client. Their eyes and mouth were sealed shut. I also tied the cloth closed with three knots while praying the Isaiah 54 V 17.

Once I had the dollie fixed, it was time to fix the feet. I turned the dollie on its head, and I placed two small hot peppers called "pico" in each foot. My petition was that if they came near my client with ill intent, they would become confused and it would become too hot for them. Like all works of this type, you have to work on justice—you can't just do this type of work because someone made you mad or you don't like the person. If you don't like them, just stay away from them. Conjure is not a free-for-all—every action causes a reaction! If you go against a target and they are innocent of any wrongdoing, you could get hit with your own work if they figure out someone is throwing at them. Be responsible for your action.

When I finished with the dollie, it was time to give it to my client. The first thing was to have my client take a black taper and wipe herself down with it, then light the candle and pray the Isaiah 54 V 17. Then I had her cleanse herself off with the dollie before we wrapped it up to be put away. I did this so the offenders could get a taste of their own works. This work is twofold: you have to not only shut their mouth but also bind them so they can cause no more harm. By doing a brush-down with the dollie, you have pulled their ugliness off of you and placed it right where it belongs—right back on them. When this work is done right, they won't even think about you.

To Stop Gossip

If someone is gossiping about you, you can draw a mouth on an egg, then write their name over the mouth. Once this is done, place an *X* over the mouth to shut it. Dress the egg with the appropriate oil, and then roll the egg in red pepper. Wrap the egg in a black cloth and place it somewhere safe. Leave it there for nine days, then take it to running water and throw it in the water. Also throw in an offering of five pennies. Every time the person says your name, their mouth will burn. It will not be long until they stop talking about you. By throwing the egg in running water you are also removing the person from you.

Saint Ramon to Stop Gossip

St. Ramon is a Spanish saint. He is worked with when you want to shut someone's mouth. St. Ramon is a very powerful saint. If he will work with you, then you have a strong protector. He is not a saint to take lightly. I have worked with him for over thirty years—he is one of my grandson's name saints. If someone is harassing you, and they just will not leave you alone, then you need to petition St. Ramon. Here is what you need:

San Ramon candle

1 penny

The person's name

A marker

A powdered herb that is used to shut people up

Light a small stick candle, place a few drops of wax over the face of St. Ramon, then stick the penny over the face with the face on the penny turned inward so it is looking at the flame of the candle. Write the person's name under the penny in a straight line down the glass. Then sprinkle the powdered herb in the candle—it only takes a pinch. More is not better because you can overload the candle and make the candle burn too fast or it could catch on fire. Say St. Ramon's novena, then call on St. Ramon to shut their mouth. Let the candle burn all the way out. This works fast. I have seen it work within three hours of lighting the candle.

QUESTIONS & ANSWERS

Q. Can I make a person love me?

A. You *can* force someone to love you, but understand you will *always* have to work on them to keep them!

Q. Is doing love work against God's laws?

A. No, it is not as long as you do divination first to see if the work can be done.

Q. Is it wrong to do enemy work?

A. It is not, as long as it is justified.

Q. Is Conjure the work of the devil?

A. No. There is no devil in this work as far as I know. I was raised to believe that we are each given choices and it depends on what we decided to do if it turns out right or wrong. My mama never preached to us about a devil—all she would say is every action causes a reaction and we alone are responsible for our actions. So, if you decided to do a work in this book, please understand that it is your responsibility to know if it is right or wrong.

Q. Are there white and black magic works in Conjure?

A. No, there is no white or black magic in Conjure. The work is simply the work, and we are each responsible for our actions.

Q. What is the difference between Conjure and Hoodoo?

A. There is no difference; they are one and the same.

Q. Is the Bible part of Conjure?

A. Yes! I know many folks have tried to remove the Bible from the work. They say that the ancestors were not Christians. I agree with that 100 percent! However, I believe that by the third generation, all of the ancestors were forced into Christianity *and* they made the Bible work for them!

Q. Do I need a lot of supplies to do this type of work?

A. You do not. You can do a successful job with as little as a prayer and a petition.

Q. Will karma come back on me for doing domination work?

A. Conjure has no law such as karma; we are all responsible for our own actions.

Q. Can I do any type of work I want to do since there is no karma or rule of three.

A. Yes, of course, you can. Just remember that any work that is done without justification has the chance of coming home to roost.

Q. Can a work backfire?

A. Yes, it can! You have to understand that part of the foundation of this work is that the work be justified. If it is *not* justified, then it can come back on the worker.

Q. Can I do a work that Spirit has warned me against doing?

A. Of course, you can. But if the work is not justified and you do it anyway, then you and you alone have to answer for any repercussions that may accrue.

Q. What can I do to build a relationship with my spirits so I can be open to what they tell me about conjure works?

A. You build a relationship with them by honoring them and talking to them.

Q. Can I do divination for myself to see if a work is justified? What do you suggest I do?

A. You should do divination before all works. You can work with cards, bones, or a pendulum.

Q. How would I approach an elder to learn more about Conjure?

A. Even now, as I write in 2020, going back home to South Carolina is just like I never left, people are still the same, the separation is still the same, and they still expect folks to know their place and to stay in it! Like I tell folks who think they can just walk up to ole folks and start asking them questions about this work, that ain't never gonna happen. If you don't believe me, take your behind on down there and see for yourself. You may go to a class folks are offering over there, but that ain't the real ole folks. You are not gonna find *them* teaching no class in town. You are gonna find them sitting on their front door stoops minding their own business—and not to be rude, but if you're white, you will be lucky if they even invite you on the porch. It is up to them if they want to share with you, plain and simple.

The very first thing they are gonna wanna know is who your people are, where you come from. Folks are very close-knit down south; they don't like strangers prowling around asking questions. It is the culture and the way of life over there. In order to understand a people, you will have to first understand where those folks come from and the condition they have lived in. The Gullah Geechee nation down there is as close as you are gonna get to the ancestors of the day.

Q. What is Conjure?

A. Conjure is magic, plain and simple. Conjure was brought over by the slaves from Africa. It is a combination of culture, beliefs, and knowledge brought over by the ancestors.

Q. Where did Conjure come from?

A. Conjure was brought to North America from Africa with the first slaves.

Q. Is it the same work that was done in the African homeland?

A. No! That was not possible. For one thing, the roots, herbs, trees, and the land in general were different. The ancestors weren't allowed to bring anything with them, so none of the things from their homeland came along with them here. Instead, they found things over here that worked for them. So the answer is no, it is not possible for it to be the same exact work.

Q. Who are the ancestors of Conjure?

A. The ancestors of Conjure are the slaves that were captured and brought here on the slave ships to be sold, carrying only their knowledge.

Q. Were the ancestors of Conjure Christians?

A. This question has caused many debates and outright battles. Some folks still refuse to accept the fact that Conjure is hidden within Christianity.

Christianity was already in Africa by the time the ancestors were captured. History tells us this. Those who were not Christians when they were captured were soon forced to become Christians, and they made Christianity work for them, as we will see over and over in this book. So to answer the question: yes, the ancestors of Conjure were Christians.

Q. Can white folks do conjure work?

A. Yes, they can, as long as they honor the ancestors of this work. Those ancestors are the folks who were kidnapped and sold into slavery. They brought this work here and deserve to be honored. And who better to honor them than white folks who at one time enslaved them?

Q. What is a two-headed worker?

A. A two-headed worker is a worker who works with both hands! This means that they can heal or curse, not just one or the other. Most conjure workers are two-headed workers.

Q. What does "justified" mean?

A. In conjure work "justified" basically means that the target has to have done you a wrong. I don't mean a slight or they made you mad; you have to have a good reason for the work. It is really important that you understand that you and you alone are responsible for your actions; so make sure you have a good reason for doing the work. Just because you don't like some-one is not a good enough reason.

Q. Do works have to be justified?

A. Yes. As a rule, any time you work on someone, the work should be justified. The "every action causes a reaction" rule works here. You can't cross someone up just because they pissed you off. That would be unjust. Also, if your target did a reversal, then you would get hit by your own work.

SWITCHING WORKS

Switching has become a thing of the past. Most of the new generation of workers do not know anything about it because the old workers aren't talking. I know I am going to hear a lot of complaints from some about the information I am sharing in this book. I already get little jabs from some—talking about "I write, but I don't give works out"—well, that is you! I write for the ancestors of this work, lest folks forget their suffering and for my mama, granddaddy, and my elders! It seems like some folks would rather the work be lost or become a jumbled hot mess like most is today rather than have it shared so it can live on! There are some old works I have been taught that I do not share and will never write about because they are too dangerous—even though any work can be dangerous in the wrong hands.

Back when I was growing up in the country, the roads were dirt and the yards were mostly dirt unless you lived in the big house and could afford to buy grass seeds to plant in the yard. My people worked in the field, so they didn't have that kind of money to waste. They were lucky they had food and the things they needed to live on. Switching was a big deal back then and a powerful work if you knew what you were doing—most folks knew about it from whispers they had heard. A lot of these works may seem too simple to do, but you have to remember there wasn't money to spend buying supplies and such. They had to work with what they had. This work is done through knowledge, prayer, petitions, determination, and faith! Don't ever be fooled by the simplicity of it!

Back when I was growing up the yards were swept. They swept them to remove any trick that might have been laid but also to remove their footprint from the dirt. Your footprint is just as strong as a personal concern, and it can be tricked just like your other personal concerns can be. I have been taught three different ways to do switching work by three different elders. I'm gonna share all three of them with you. I've worked all three over the years with great success. The first one I was ever taught was switching a foot track. Some workers say to work with a weeping willow switch, and others say a small oak branch because the oak is powerful. Others say it doesn't matter what kind of switch you use. I think the weeping willow is my favorite because it is said to make the target weep.

It's hard nowadays to gather a dirt footprint because of all the concrete laid everywhere, but if you can find one, then you can switch it. Switching work is done to punish the target. It is believed that when you are switching the footprint you are switching the person. Some ole folks say if you can get where they stepped, all you have to do is switch the footprint because it *is* the target. I was taught to say a prayer and my petition over the print before switching it. At the end of this section you will find some prayers you can work with for this. I'm going to share my favorites for each of the works. You also need to work with the track either coming or going. Are you trying to draw them in? Then you work with the track that is coming toward you. If you are sending them away from you, then you work the track that is going away. This is very important or you might send a target away you wanted to bring to you.

If the target has harmed you and you wish to give them a taste of their own medicine, you need a weeping willow switch and their footprint. Pray Nahum 1 V 3 along with your petition over the footprint and switch it really good. Repeat the prayers and petition at least three times. You can gather up some of the print and place it in a medicine bottle to be able to keep working it.

The next work is done to move someone out. This is one of my favorites, and it works fast. I have done this work many times over the last thirty years since our old neighbor Ms. Johnny had to move out of the house behind us. The owner of the house just rents to anyone, and they seem to always be disrespectful and noisy. We have some neighbors now as of this writing I am fixing to help on their way! They keep us up all hours of the night drinking and fighting, so they gotta go! If you have a problem like this, you can get the dirt from the front door or the driveway. Place the dirt, red ant dirt, and the ash from Deuteronomy 11 V 10 in a white handkerchief and tie it in a knot while praying the Deuteronomy 11 V 10 and your petition over the knot. Then you whip it with an oak stick while praying the prayer and your petition over the packet. Continue the work daily until they move. Once they move out, burn the packet and blow the ash to the east with a blessing that they find peace.

Sometimes you simply have to nail a target down. Place the dirt from their track in an old sock. You can go to the thrift store and find an old pair of socks. Take the left sock and mix the dirt with the ash from Job 13 V 27 together and place it in the sock. Pray your petition and the Job 13 V 27 over the sock, and on the third prayer pull the knot tight. Take a willow switch and switch them good. Continue to do the work until you are satisfied that justice has been served, or never let them out—that is up to you. If you choose to set them free, then burn the sock and plant the ashes under a tree facing the east.

To Give Them a Taste of Their Own Medicine

Nahum 1 V 3
The Lord is slow to anger and great in power,
And the Lord will by no means leave the guilty
    unpunished. In whirlwind and storm is His
    way,
And clouds are the dust beneath His feet.
Psalm 89 V 51
With which Your enemies have reproached, O
    Lord, With which they have reproached the
    footsteps of Your anointed.

To Move Them Out

Deuteronomy 11 V 10
For the land, into which you are entering to pos-
    sess it, is not like the land of Egypt from which
    you came, where you used to sow your seed
    and water it with your foot like a vegetable
    garden.
Proverbs 7 V 11
She is boisterous and rebellious,
Her feet do not remain at home.

To Nail Them Down

Job 13 V 27
You put my feet in the stocks
And watch all my paths;
You set a limit for the soles of my feet,

For Crossing a Target

Acts 5 V 9
Then Peter said to her, "Why is it that you have
agreed together to put the Spirit of the Lord
to the test? Behold, the feet of those who have
buried your husband are at the door, and they
will carry you out as well."

PRAYERS

I'm going to share some additional chapters and verses from the Bible here that will help your work be a success. All you have to do is put them to good use. I'm not going to write out the verses for you. Get a Bible and read them.

I know a lot of folks grit their teeth when they are told Conjure is built around the Bible, the Psalms, the saints, and prayers. Well, it is. These things *make up* conjure work! So if you want to be a worker, open up this great book and search for the things that are there to help you achieve what you need in life.

I know that some of you who read this will say, "I don't read the Bible! I am not Christian; I don't believe in the church! I don't want to have anything to do with the Bible!" I have heard this and more numerous times from my students and from others.

I say, "Stop right there!" Forget about all the rules of the church, all the man-made rules. Really look at the Bible for what it is—a work of power! Words hold power; prayer holds power! Forget everything else, but that the words written in this book we call the Bible *hold power!*

Conjure is built around this great book and the wisdom it holds. If you remove the Bible from conjure work, then what you are doing really isn't conjure work! It becomes something else. If you can hold the greatest conjure book ever written in your hands and learn the power from it, why in the world would you let anyone stop you?

Below you will find some of the chapters and verses I depend on in my work.

For Deliverance

2 Samuel 22 V 2-4

2 Samuel 22 V 5-25

2 Samuel 22 V 48-51

2 Kings 19 V 19

Psalm 18 V 3-19

Psalm 71 V 3-5

Proverbs 11 V 1-6

Proverbs 11 V 8-9

Jeremiah 15 V 15-17

Jeremiah 39 V 17-18

Zephaniah 3 V 17-20

Spiritual Weapons

Psalm 120 V 1-7

Psalm 144 V 1-2

Isaiah 8 V 9-10

Joel 3 V 9-10

2 Corinthians 6 V 4-10

Ephesians 6 V 10-18

Victory

Numbers 10 V 9

Psalm 7 V 13-16

Psalm 44 V 5-8

Proverbs 21 V 31

Reversal Work

Psalm 7 V 13-16

Success

Joshua 1 V 5-9

Job 36 V 7-11

Psalm 1 V 1-3

Psalm 92 V 12-15

Psalm 118 V 5-17

Isaiah 60 V 17-21

Jeremiah 1 V 7-10

Prosperity

Genesis 30 V 43

Genesis 49 V 22-26

Deuteronomy 8 V 11-18

2 Chronicles 31 V 10

Psalm 112 V 1-9

Proverbs 8 V 18-21

Proverbs 10 V 22-24

Ezekiel 36 V 29-30

Nahum 2 V 2-9

2 Corinthians 9 V 5-15

Protection

Numbers 23 V 23-24

Deuteronomy 33 V 27-29

1 Chronicles 16 V 21-24

Job 1 V 10

Proverbs 1 V 33

Ezekiel 34 V 11-12

Ezekiel 34 V 23-27

Joel 3 V 16

Zachariah 9 V 8

Luke 21 V 17-19

Romans 16 V 17-20

Prayers Against Your Enemy

I wanted to add some extra prayers that can help when you are dealing with folks who don't leave others alone. Below you will find various prayers from the Bible that can be worked with when you are dealing with an enemy. Like the Psalms, these prayers have the power to drive your enemies away from you and defeat them. There are many of these types of prayers in the Bible. Sometimes you can find full works in the Bible that give you step-by-step instruction on how to make things happen like the Joshua 6 tearing down of the walls of Jericho.

You don't have to do full works all the time, though. Sometimes just a prayer and your petition will be enough if you do consecutive days of prayer.

ISAIAH 54 V 17

No weapon that is formed against thee shall prosper; and every tongue that shall rise against thee in judgment thou shalt condemn. This is the heritage of the servants of the Lord, and their righteousness is of me, saith the Lord.

LUKE 1 V 74

That he would grant unto us, that we being delivered out of the hand of our enemies might serve him without fear.

PSALM 27 V 5-6

5 For in the time of trouble he shall hide me in his pavilion: in the secret of his tabernacle shall he hide me; he shall set me up upon a rock.

6 And now shall mine head be lifted up above mine enemies round about me: Therefore will I offer in his tabernacle sacrifices of joy; I will sing praises unto the Lord.

JEREMIAH 39 V 17-18

17 But I will deliver thee, in that day, saith the Lord: and thou shalt not be given into the hand of the men of whom thou art afraid.

18 For I will surely deliver thee, and thou shalt
not fall by the sword, but thy life shall be for
a prey unto thee: because thou hast put thy
trust in me, saith the Lord.

2 KINGS 17 V 39
But the Lord your God ye shall fear; and he
shall deliver you out of the hand of all your
enemies.

ISAIAH 41 V 11-12
11 Behold, all they that were incensed against
thee shall be ashamed and confounded: they
shall be as nothing; and they that strive with
thee shall perish.
12 Thou shalt seek them, and shalt not find them,
even them that contended with thee: they that
war against thee shall be as nothing, and as a
thing of nought.

PROVERBS 3 V 25-26
25 Be not afraid of sudden fear, neither of the
desolation of the wicked, when it cometh.
26 For the Lord shall be thy confidence, and shall
keep thy foot from being taken.

LUKE 1 V 71
That we should be saved from our enemies and
from the hand of all that hate us.

ACTS 18 V 10

For I am with thee, and no other man shall set on
thee to hurt thee: for I have much people in
this city.

HEBREWS 13 V 6

So that we may lay boldly say, the Lord is my
helper, and I will not fear what man shall do
unto me.

CONCLUSION

B efore I leave you to your own work, I'll share one more thing. This is something you can do to bless and bring success to someone you love.

A Bonus Work to Bring Success

There are times when you might want to bring a blessing to someone, but you know they are very proud and would be insulted by the offer. There are still ways you can bless them without insulting them. We call this work tricks for a reason. If you do divination and Spirit gives you the okay, you can trick a stone you picked up from their yard or drive; you could even pick up a stick out of their yard to bless. Anything can be worked with to cross or bless a target.

For this work you need a rock from their home, dirt from the four corners of a crossroads, some sugar, shredded money, and a magnet. Place the rock in a glass bowl, set the magnet on top of the rock to draw and then cover the magnet with the dirt from the crossroads. For five days burn a white stick candle in the bowl. Say your prayers over the candle for the roads to be open for the target, and petition the owner of the crossroads to open the roads. This is very personal, and you speak the prayer from your heart.

Once the five days are up, you add the money and the sugar to the bowl. On the sixth day you will burn another white stick candle and repeat the prayers and petition. You will continue to work the bowl until you have reached a total of twenty-one days; so that is five days the first set of burns then another sixteen burns one a day to make the twenty-one days. Once all the candles have been burned, you take the rock and put it back in the yard. The rest of the ingredients are taken to the crossroads closest to the target's home and poured in the center of the crossroads with twenty-one pennies as an offering to the spirit that sits in the crossroads.

In Closing

I have to say this before I close out the book: Always work the way you feel comfortable working. Do not let anyone tell you how to do your work. I have been working for a little over forty years and have learned that you have to be at home with the way you work. There is nothing written in stone. Conjure has been passed down over the years through families. No two families were taught to work the same. You will find if you talk to rootworkers, there are many different ways to do the same trick. None of them are right, but none of them are wrong either. That is the way they were taught to do the work. What I am trying to say is—find what works for you. Do not worry about how Bob, Betty, or Joe does the job. If it works for you, then that is what matters.

—Starr

LIST OF HERBS AND ROOTS

Basil (*Ocimum basilicum*)

Bay leaf (*Laurus nobilis*)

Black mustard (*Brassica nigra*)

Calamus (*Acorus calamus*)

Cinnamon (*Cinnamomum zeylanicum*)

Devil's shoestrings (*Viburnum spp*)

Frankincense (*Boswellia carterii*)

Ginger (*Zingiber officinale*)

Heal-all (*Prunella vulgaris*)

High John root/High John the Conqueror root (*Convolvulus jalapa, Ipomoea jalapa, I. purga*)

Jezebel root (*Iris fulva, I. foliosa, I. hexagona, I. tectorum*)

Lavender (*Lavandula stoechas*)

Licorice root (*Glycyrrhiza glabra*)

Lovage (*Levisticum officinale*)

Master of the Woods (*Galium odoratum*)

Master root (*Imperatoria ostruthium*)

Pico pepper (*Capsicum spp.*)

Poppy (*Papaver spp.*)

Queen Elizabeth root (*Iris germanica*)

Red pepper (*Capsicum spp.*)

Rosemary (*Rosmarinus officinalis*)

Roses (*Rosa spp.*)

Saffron (*Crocus sativa*)

Self heal (*Prunella vulgaris*)

Slippery elm (*Ulmus fulva*)

Solomon's seal (*Polygonatum multiflorum*)

Spikenard (*Nardostachys jatamans*)

ABOUT THE AUTHOR

STARR CASAS holds onto the values of her ancestors. A traditional Conjure woman and veteran rootworker for more than forty years, Mama Starr is a prolific author and hands-on teacher, who presents workshops throughout the United States. She also owns the store Mama Starr's Style LLC in Houston. Find her online at *oldstyleconjure.com* and on Instagram *@starrcasas*

TO OUR READERS

Weiser Books, an imprint of Red Wheel/Weiser, publishes books across the entire spectrum of occult, esoteric, speculative, and New Age subjects. Our mission is to publish quality books that will make a difference in people's lives without advocating any one particular path or field of study. We value the integrity, originality, and depth of knowledge of our authors.

Our readers are our most important resource, and we appreciate your input, suggestions, and ideas about what you would like to see published.

Visit our website at *www.redwheelweiser.com*, where you can learn about our upcoming books and free downloads, and also find links to sign up for our newsletter and exclusive offers.

You can also contact us at *info@rwwbooks.com* or at

Red Wheel/Weiser, LLC
65 Parker Street, Suite 7
Newburyport, MA 01950